Cellar Girl

Cellar Girl

**Kidnapped and abused by
a serial killer. This is my story.**

JOSEFINA RIVERA

EBURY
PRESS

3 5 7 9 10 8 6 4

First published in 2013 by Ebury Press, an imprint of Ebury Publishing
A Random House Group company

Written with Katy Weitz

The Random House Group Limited Reg. No. 954009
Addresses for companies within the Random House Group can be found at
www.randomhouse.co.uk

A CIP catalogue record for this book is available from the British Library

The Random House Group Limited supports the Forest Stewardship
Council® (FSC®), the leading international forest-certification organisation.
Our books carrying the FSC label are printed on FSC®-certified paper.
FSC is the only forest-certification scheme supported by the leading
environmental organisations, including Greenpeace. Our paper procurement
policy can be found at www.randomhouse.co.uk/environment

Typeset by seagulls.net

Printed and bound by CPI Group (UK) Ltd, Croydon, CR0 4YY

ISBN 9780091955717

To buy books by your favourite authors and register for offers visit
www.randomhouse.co.uk

This book is dedicated to Florence Patterson, my mom, for all her strength, encouragement and discipline that helped me endure.

To Chris Lyle, for not standing in front of me or behind me but beside me through the aftermath.

And to God, for bringing me through it all.

I'm not going to allow what I see hinder what I believe.

(Anon)

Contents

Contents

Prologue

I wander along the seashore, my eyes scanning the beach. I'm looking for sea glass. In my pocket are three pieces I have found already – one is small and green, another is a curved white shard, edges worn down, and the third, a thick blue circle, has bumps on one side like the bottom of a bottle. My fingers rub at the frosted glass in my pocket as the gusty sea breeze whips at my hair and lashes at my cheeks. I inhale deeply – the salty air fills my lungs, carries away all my thoughts and lets me walk on, free to search the shore.

The pieces of glass are from old ships. Ships that once sailed the Atlantic Ocean, ships that broke down and threw stuff overboard: wine, jars, plates, glasses and bottles. The glass sank to the bottom of the ocean and during the tide, it was tossed and rolled around the seabed, over and over the sand, until the sharp fragments were worn down into smooth rounded pieces. And during high tide the sea brings in these little jewels, these fragments from another place and time. The mistier, more opaque the glass, the older it is.

I started collecting sea glass three years ago when I moved to Atlantic City, the place I now call my home. I'd always loved walking along the beach, the vast ocean beside me, lapping at my feet. The constancy of the tide I found relaxed me, made me calm. Whatever mood I was in, the sea would echo it back to me, whether I felt good, bad, sad or angry. I could walk the beach for hours, even during fierce storms when the rain came at me from every angle, driven by a punishing wind that stung my face and legs and the sea was whipped into a frothy, bubbling foam. But when I started to spot the sea glass, I felt compelled to pick them up, to rescue them and take them home. I have whole jars filled with glass. They are the tiny remnants of another life that remind me of who I am.

Like me, the sea glass has been worn down over time, its rough edges smoothed out, shaped and moulded by the tumbling oceans and shifting sands. And it is the very act of being battered and bashed about that has made these tiny discarded slivers of glass so beautiful. They have survived, they have endured the very worst that Mother Nature could throw at them and still they have come ashore. A reminder that life goes on. I look for them and I gather them up like treasure. A bounty of broken beauty only I can truly appreciate.

Out here, near the ocean, I feel peaceful, anchored. And I am finally strong enough to tell my story. The real story, the whole story, the true story. For many years I tried to forget, tried to block out of my mind all those months I spent chained in that cellar in North Marshall Street. But you don't forget, you never forget. In some ways I envy Gary Heidnik, the man who raped, beat and tortured me and five other girls, who killed two of them. Heidnik gets to rest in peace.

There is very little peace in my mind. Just these quiet moments walking along the beach. Not a day goes by when I don't think about those four months of hell I endured at Gary Heidnik's hands. Reminders are everywhere. Small, seemingly innocent things can set off a thought in my head that takes me back there.

I can walk outside and a crack of lightning will scare me enough to send me scurrying back indoors for comfort. Or I'll cross a street and see some workmen digging out a hole in the road and my heart will freeze in my chest.

These things don't mean anything to most people. But they're enough to cause me endless sleepless nights, a panic attack or at worst months of depression when I can't even get out of bed.

I may be free but in many ways I'm still chained to Heidnik. And to the dark, difficult memories of what went on in that basement while the rest of the world went on as normal.

Since then of course nothing in my life has been normal and every aspect of Heidnik's horrific crimes has been picked and pored over in detail by countless strangers. Thousands of words have been written about what happened – some true, some not.

Now I want to set the record straight so that people can judge for themselves what I did in that basement and what I felt I had to do in order to survive and to get the rest of the girls out.

Everything I did was to one end – survival, for myself and the others. As far as I could see, there was no choice, only necessity. And every single minute of every day I was down there, I knew it could be my last on this earth.

And even though I escaped, I know I'll never truly get away from Heidnik, not really.

At least I'm here to feel this torment, I tell myself. At least I have my health, my faith, my family and a million different reasons to feel grateful. Like my pieces of glass, I have been changed, shaped by the world into which I was thrown.

So now I'm ready to face what happened – I'm ready to go back to the cellar, to go back to the hole and relive every moment of torture that he put me through.

Would you have done the same in my situation? Could you have done what I did? I don't think any of us can know how we will react under such extreme circumstances until we are there, living through them.

So I don't ask you not to judge me – I know I'll be living with other people's judgments for the rest of my life, and long after I am gone. It doesn't bother me because I know only God will judge me in the end and I've never been ashamed of what I did.

Walk with me now down those dark, foreboding steps, cross over into an alternative reality where nothing makes sense anymore and the rules of normal life simply don't apply.

Take a journey with me now into the very depths of hell.

And then ask yourself, what would you have done?

Chapter One
Taken

I cradled my tiny boy in my arm, stroking his head and whispering to him: 'How you doing, my little man? You feeling okay today?'

He slept soundly in my embrace and I touched the tip of my forefinger to his squat nose then traced round his full, thick lips, just like mine.

He looked perfect, just perfect, in his sky-blue romper suit. I sighed. Just an hour earlier I'd come to the Intensive Care Nursery in the Pennsylvania Hospital in Philly's city center where he was staying while he was getting up his strength. He'd been born early, just like my other kids, so he was tiny, like a little doll. I'd bathed him and changed him as he'd squirmed irritably in my arms.

When he was all clean and dry, I gave him a bottle and halfway through the feed, he'd dropped off. I placed him gently in his see-through plastic cot and his legs splayed open in complete peacefulness. I pulled up his soft cotton blanket and just stared at him.

Now five weeks old, Ricky's skinny arms were beginning to fill out and his small, trusting fingers wrapped themselves unconsciously around my own.

Ricky was my third child but I knew that getting him back home to live with me was no longer my decision. I would have to prove to child protective services that I was a good mom, someone willing to put my children's needs before my own.

Ricky, you see, had been born with drugs in his system.

Tears sprang to my eyes now as I made a heartfelt, silent promise to my sleeping child.

I will do the right thing by you, Ricky. I'll clean up my act. I'll get the other kids back. We'll all be a family. I promise. Momma will make things right again. You'll see.

He was so content, so innocent I couldn't help feeling overwhelmed with guilt and sorrow at the way I'd brought him into this world.

He didn't ask to be born this way – it was my fault. I knew that.

Just a year ago everything was going so well – I'd been clean from drugs for a while, I had my two girls and I was living with the man I loved.

How quickly everything had unraveled. Working during the day, I'd left my sister Iris in charge of the kids. What I didn't know at the time was that she was out most of the time, getting high. When the neighbors discovered her kids running wild up and down the streets unsupervised they'd stopped the eldest boy and asked him where his mom was.

'I don't know,' came back the honest reply. That's when child protective services swooped in. They took

Iris's three kids and my youngest daughter Zornae, who was just a year old at the time, and I had to find a new place to live.

Thankfully they left LaToya, my five-year-old daughter from a previous relationship. But months later Toya, or Bookie, as I called her, was snatched by her father. By then my relationship with Zornae's father was also beginning to break down and I was pregnant with Ricky. Everything was a mess. To my eternal shame, I fell back on the bad habits that had plagued me since I was a teenager: smoking crack and hustling.

I will go into the full details of how this sorry mess came to be later on, but for now all you need to know is that I was a vulnerable child, in an environment where taking drugs was the norm, who had found something that blocked out all the badness in the world and I was hooked. So hooked it stopped me being the mother I wanted to be. My addiction came before anything else. If had my time again, I'd never have tried crack. It ruined my life, ruined it in the worst possible way.

Now I looked down at Ricky and told myself: *you will fix this, Josefina. You have to fix this.*

I left the hospital that day and returned to my new apartment. This place meant everything to me. It was going to be the place I could reunite my family. I'd fixed it up real nice, with bunk beds for the girls and a cot for Ricky. The date had been fixed in court when child protective services would visit to approve my new home.

Now I just needed a little more time to get off the drugs and everything would be okay. I made myself a cheese and ham sandwich then took a bath.

It was November 26, 1986, the day before Thanksgiving. I just needed some cash to see me through the holidays, to tide me over, keep me from rattling. So I switched off the TV, turned off the lights and went outside.

* * *

'Are you dating?' the man asked.

It was around 9 p.m. and I was out walking the streets, looking for a customer so yeah, that's what I was doing, dating.

I wore my usual black jeans, leather jacket, a black T-shirt and sneakers. I never had to dress up to pick up guys. Naturally slim with full lips and prominent cheekbones, I always found it easy to get work. I'd put on a bouffant wig over my ponytail this evening and pulled my jacket tight to keep out the early winter chill.

Tonight was no different from any other night of the week, apart from the fact that it was the night before Thanksgiving so there weren't many cars going up and down Front Street, Philadelphia. Still, it couldn't have been more than ten minutes before I noticed a car pass and then turn round at the bottom of the street.

That's good, he was probably coming back to pick me up, I figured. I didn't relish the idea of being out in the cold for long.

A tan Cadillac Seville pulled up alongside me – a nice car, an expensive car.

Then the window came down and the guy asked me if I was dating.

It was my very first look at Gary Heidnik.

And all I noticed was a pair of bright, very piercing blue eyes – so pale and translucent you felt you could see right through them and into his skull. Except you weren't looking at him. He had *you* in his stare.

Other than those eyes, there was nothing unusual about this guy. Nothing at all.

He was white, with an ordinary face – straight nose, square jaw, wavy brown hair and a trimmed beard. He was slim and wore a brown cowhide jacket with fringing down the arms. Just a regular guy.

'Yeah,' I replied.

'I want to do something. Will you come back to mine?'

'I don't go back to other people's houses,' I said. I had to have a few ground rules and this was one of them.

'Well, I'm six feet tall so it's kind of hard for me to do stuff in the car,' he said and I peered into the car. Leather upholstery, clean and fresh smelling. It's true, he had long legs but still I was reluctant. I didn't have many rules in this line of work but it's one I'd usually been quite strict about. After all, you didn't want to waste time driving to and from someone's house when you could be back out working again in ten minutes if you gave them what they wanted in a parking lot.

But I could feel the temperature dropping around me.

'Come on,' he urged. 'I'll give you fifty bucks.'

'How far is it?' I asked.

'Only about fifteen minutes' drive. Come on, we'll be done in half an hour then I'll drop you back.'

'Okay.'

Fifty bucks – it was enough to make my night worthwhile and then I could get back to the warmth of my apartment. Get a hit, get high and relax. And think about getting my kids in the morning. If only I hadn't. If only I had tried to get clean that night. It would have worked out better for us all.

I slid into the passenger seat next to him and as we started to drive he asked me if I had kids.

'Sure,' I said. 'That's why I can't be long – I've got the babysitter back home minding my kids, so if I'm late she's on golden time.'

It wasn't true but I wanted to be clear from the start that I wasn't going to be hanging around afterwards.

'What's your name?' I asked as we sped through the dark, empty streets.

'Gary,' he said. 'What's yours?'

'I'm Nicole,' I told him. This was my working name – I didn't like to use my real name Josefina Rivera while I was out on the streets. For some reason it felt uncomfortable, so when I was hooking, I called myself Nicole.

We headed through to the slum district of Philly and soon we pulled through a waist-high chain-link fence into a yard. We'd arrived at his home – 3520 North Marshall Street.

He took me in through the front porch. It was very dark outside and in the house too. This wasn't a good neighborhood – lots of drug dealers, deadbeats and burnt-out cars. It got itself a reputation recently as the 'OK Corral' of Philly thanks to a gang shoot-out. Still, I didn't mind. I'd been pretty much everywhere and thanks to my own drug habit, I was used to seeing the seedier side of life.

Crack was my drug – always uppers, never downers. At first it had started out as a bit of fun. When you're young, you think you're invincible, you never imagine becoming so hooked on something that it's all you can think about. You never imagine being driven to extreme lengths to get a hit. Or that you'd put drugs before a life growing inside you. And for me, somewhere along the line crack had taken over. It wasn't a choice anymore. Crack had become the only way to get through the day. I needed a hit first thing in the morning or I couldn't move at all. It didn't matter how much money I made, I always spent it all. If I made $50 or $500 I could always be sure of one thing – by the next day it would be gone and I'd be back out on the streets.

Gary led the way inside. I briefly looked around to see we were in a living room with a couch and TV and a few rugs on the floor. We walked through to a dark dining room with a pinball machine, dining chairs and dining table. It was a normal, regular house as far as I could see. The only thing that struck me as peculiar was the fact that instead of wallpaper, he'd stuck something unusual on the walls: money.

He'd glued dimes, nickels and quarters all around the walls of the dining room. And in the kitchen the walls were covered with pennies. Jeez, why would anyone do that? It looked like it must have taken hours.

He led me upstairs to his bedroom and on the wall along the staircase and all along the corridor upstairs there were more dollar bills. Occasionally there was a $20 bill, I guess just to make it interesting. Maybe he was showing off. Letting the world know he's got enough dough to paint his house with the stuff.

Gary took me into his bedroom where I started undressing. He handed me my $50 and I noticed as I was getting on the bed that it was angled so that my head pointed downwards. He explained he had a lung problem and it helped him while he slept. He waited till I was lying on the bed then he pulled off his jeans and shorts but kept his lumberjack shirt on, before climbing on top of me.

Without saying a word he put himself inside me and started pumping away rhythmically. He didn't say a word, just pounded on top of me with quickening thrusts until he was through. To me, this was business as usual. The quicker the better as far as I was concerned.

I got up to put my clothes on and it was then, just as I was about to step into my knickers, that I felt his arm come around my throat from behind, choking me.

Oh my God!

I wanted to scream but I couldn't, I couldn't even breathe. He was choking the air out of me and there was nothing that could pass through into my lungs.

I started to panic. Images from my life whipped through my mind, spinning and flipping past my eyes, giving me one last brief glimpse at the life I was about to leave behind. My mom, my children, the men I'd loved and lost…

It felt like I was going to pass out but I was afraid that if I lost consciousness, I'd never regain it. So I was struggling and bucking under him.

Suddenly, I felt him relax his grip a little and I gasped for breath.

He pulled one of my arms behind me and I heard a click as he attached a handcuff to my wrist. I started wriggling again, desperately trying to twist my body to get away from him. Whatever he had in mind, this couldn't be good.

'Stop struggling or I'm going to choke you again,' he said gruffly. 'Just put your other arm behind your back.'

He tone was calm, matter-of-fact – there wasn't any anger or annoyance in his voice at all. It was as if he was giving me instructions on how to boil a kettle. That tone of voice was even more chilling to me. What was this all about? A million nightmare scenarios ran through my head.

He had my arm in a tight grip and I knew he wasn't messing around so I put my other hand behind my back and he cuffed that hand.

Naked and handcuffed, I was led downstairs into the

living room, through to the dining room and over to a door that led down some steps into his basement.

No man had ever been physically violent with me before. I'd never experienced anything like this. I was frightened. Very frightened.

Gary clamped my arms tightly behind me and pushed me roughly down the steps. The glare of a bare light bulb hanging from the ceiling illuminated a stark, sparse room. There was a large freezer down there, a radio blaring out music, another pinball machine and in the midst of all this normality, I saw that he'd dug a hole in the ground.

When I saw the hole, my heart starting thumping even harder and my body became rigid with fear. What was this hole for? Was he going to kill me? Was this my grave?

I was in complete shock, terrified, cold, gasping for breath and praying these weren't my last seconds on earth.

As I stood there, Gary started to put on these muffler clamps round my ankles. They looked like the kind of clamps that are used to attach the exhaust pipe to the bottom of the car – one straight side attached to a half circle.

He screwed the clamps on tight then he applied Krazy Glue on the screws and tightened them up again. He was working methodically, diligently, and it seemed as if he knew exactly what he was doing. There was nothing panicked or rushed about his movements. Finally he took out a hairdryer and dried the glue with the dryer.

It was bizarre, seeing this ordinary-looking appliance being used in such a sick, twisted way.

I was standing there, naked, my hands cuffed behind me, in complete shock.

Eventually when he finished his work, he attached the clamps to a long chain that he clamped to a sewer pipe along the wall of the basement with a padlock.

Finally he undid my cuffs and pushed me into the hole.

The hole was too small for my five-foot-six-inch frame and I didn't fit. So he kept pushing my head down. At some point my wig must have fallen off because he was pushing hard down onto my ponytail. I was squashed against the bare, cold earth and my legs were folded up so that my chin was resting on my knees, one arm curled around my head while the other was locked to my side. I was screaming with agony and protest but Gary just carried on as if nothing in the world could stop him. He didn't even bother to tell me to shut up. The radio was so loud it completely drowned out my shouts.

Once I was in the hole Gary pulled a heavy board over the top. I watched with horror as he pushed the board slowly across the hole, inch by inch until suddenly I was in complete darkness, alone and more frightened than I ever had been in my life.

I smelled the dense, earthy soil around me and tried my best to wriggle my body so that I wasn't squashed so awkwardly but Gary must have put something heavy on top of the board to weigh it down because, as hard as I tried to push against it, it was clamped tight, like a lid.

The next thing I heard was the heavy sound of footsteps on the wooden steps that led from the basement to the ground floor. He was going back upstairs. He was leaving me here. I was overwhelmed by panic. What if he was going to leave me here to rot? What if he left me here forever? What if the air ran out?

I started to cry and whimper, petrified.

Oh God. Oh God – what's happening to me?

I had to get out. I had to!

I started yelling: 'Let me out! Let me out! Help! Get me out of here! Somebody call the cops. I'm being kept prisoner!'

I yelled and yelled and yelled for hours. But nothing happened, no one came and there I was, stuck in that same twisted position the whole time, screaming and hollering for my life. My arm went numb after a while and the cold earth chilled me to the very bone.

Occasionally I stopped to listen for a sign that someone could hear me but in those moments I felt the terror grip me and I'd start to sob again. So I'd start shouting again. It was all I could think to do.

Chapter Two
The Hole

Music. I could hear music.

I heard it coming from far away and recognized the song – it was Anita Baker's 'Caught up in the Rapture'. They'd been playing this same song on the radio on and off for hours.

My arms and legs were so stiff I could barely feel them; all I could feel was the coldness of my skin against the damp, gritty earth.

My mind was foggy – where was I?

I'd woken up in a world I didn't recognize – my limbs were curled awkwardly around my body, darkness was everywhere and the bitter, iron taste of blood was in my parched mouth.

The ground had enclosed me completely – it was underneath me, around me, on every side and the smell was like the ground after it rained, just closer. Much closer.

I could feel my cheeks were damp – had I been crying in my sleep? I couldn't tell. Maybe something was trickling from my eye – it felt sore.

I blinked myself awake and tried to focus on my

surroundings but my vision refused to cooperate. There was no light, just darkness.

I had been buried alive.

* * *

Today was Thanksgiving. I knew that because I heard the radio announcers cheerily report that it was 6 a.m., then 7 a.m., and 8 a.m. And so on until it was now 9 p.m. I'd been down here for twenty-four hours already – a whole day had passed since Gary led me down here in handcuffs.

How on earth did I end up in this godforsaken place, not knowing whether I would live from one moment to the next?

I should be at home. Why was I here?

I thought of my mom, Florence Patterson – she'd be expecting me to call today. If I didn't call, she'd worry, like any mother would.

Florence wasn't my birth mother but she was my mom in every other sense. She'd taken me in after my birth parents left me and my older brother and sister in an apartment to die.

They just walked out and left us when I was six weeks old.

We were only rescued because the neighbors heard me crying and called the police. If they hadn't alerted the police, nobody would have found us.

When the police knocked down the door they found me, my two-year-old sister Iris and my one-year-old brother Freddy in a pitiful state – freezing, cold and hungry.

Afterwards, when the police tried to trace my parents, the neighbors said they hadn't seen them in a real long while. Who knew how long we were there? Or how many times we'd been left like that.

We were placed in temporary foster homes before I went to live with my beautiful mom and dad when I was four months old. And that's where I stayed until my early twenties.

Down in the hole, I started weeping. *Mom! Will I see my mom again?*

I loved my mom so much I never wanted to be apart from her. By the time I arrived in their home, Florence and Augustus had already brought up eight of their own kids so me and my other foster sister Althea were spoiled rotten. Thanks to a wealth of hand-me-downs we got everything we could ever want and more – toys, clothes, trips and treats.

We had a living room that stretched out for one whole floor of the house, and it was stacked full of toys. And I'd be having a temper tantrum looking for a missing toy when most kids my age would be happy with just one of the toys I had!

Mom and I didn't look anything alike: she was short and black while my birth mother was Mexican and my birth father was Puerto Rican. Back then child protective services didn't bother with us being the same color as our fostering family. The important thing was getting in a loving home and in that regard I was blessed.

Mom was heavy but she wasn't fat. She had her hair done in curls most days, wore glasses and always made herself look nice. Most of all, she was very mannerly and polite and didn't put up with no nonsense from me! Having brought up eight kids before I was even born, she knew her way around child-rearing.

The only thing she wasn't prepared for was how sick I was as a child. Thanks to my bad start in life, I had pneumonia as a baby and it was really serious.

At just a few months old my fever got so high so that I had to be taken to the hospital.

It was tough for Mom – a couple of times they called her in, saying I wasn't going to last the night, but somehow, somehow I always pulled through.

'You're a little fighter!' my mom would laugh as I got older.

The pneumonia would continue to plague me through-out my childhood, until eventually the hospital stopped admitting me and just gave my mom the medicine to administer at home.

Mom was always ready with a comforting bowl of soup as I lay in bed, huddled under the covers as the fever seared through my body.

Even today I suffer from asthma, respiratory weakness and whole host of allergies.

We grew up in a good area of Philly called the Museum District, and my parents were God-fearing folk so we always went to mass every single morning. As a young kid, I'd be so bored I couldn't sit still. I'd be crawling up and around the pews, making trouble and generally misbehaving.

And every single morning, after getting back from church, Mom would give me a whooping for my bad behavior.

Yeah, Mom was strict – she made sure we all could read and write before we started school and we all knew how to cook and clean and wash after ourselves even though she did it for us most of the time. We had chores, like making our beds, and after meals, my sister would wash up and I'd dry. There wasn't a lot of time to be sitting around, doing nothing.

In the whole time I was at home I only said I was bored once, and on that occasion my mom quickly replied: 'Oh really? You bored? Well, that's good because I got a lot of things you can be getting on with like scrubbing this floor to start with!'

I looked at the huge kitchen floor and set to work getting it all clean. Once I thought I had it looking nice I called her back in, all swollen up with pride. But Mom had high standards and she didn't settle for anything less.

'Well!' she exclaimed, a steely glint in her eye, 'now you got the dirt all spread around evenly, you can start cleaning it up!'

I was cleaning the damn floor for hours that day!

Back in the hole, I sobbed as I remembered Mom's love for me, and how she had always wanted to do the best thing by me.

One day when I was three years old my birth father turned up.

It must have all been arranged because when I got up that morning, Mom said: 'You're going to have a visitor today. What do you want to wear?'

I picked out my favorite dress – a red one with white lace trim.

Mom put the dress on me and did my hair all nice.

It wasn't long before a strange-looking man turned up. He sat on the couch, my mom sat in a chair facing him and I stood at her shoulder, leaning into her, too shy to speak or even look at this guy.

'Why don't you talk to him?' Mom kept saying. 'That's your dad.'

I shook my head. Who was this man? He wasn't my dad. He was nothing to do with me. I just wanted him to go away so we could go back to being normal and playing.

Eventually, after exhausting himself trying to get me to say something, that strange-looking man turned to my mom. 'This girl needs to get her butt whipped because she doesn't listen to anything anybody says.'

Mom pursed her lips and with a gentle turn of her head, said: 'Well, it won't get done here.'

He left not long after that and Mom took me into the kitchen and stood me on a chair so she could take my nice dress off and put me into my play clothes.

As she pulled the pretty red dress up over my head I found my voice again: 'I love you, Mommy!'

She looked at me with exasperation in her eyes, but said nothing.

Then: 'You know, you have another mommy out there somewhere.'

'No I don't. I love you.'

'I love you too. Now go outside and play.'

After that my dad returned to see me one more time but I had mumps so he couldn't come in my room. Later, in our teens, me and my real sister Iris would seek out my father in an effort to trace our birth mother.

Mom didn't hide the fact that I was fostered – she wanted me to know the truth so I would be prepared one day in case my parents wanted me back in their lives.

That was Mom – she didn't sugar-coat a thing. She was direct, to the point, said what needed to be said and then moved on. There wasn't any tiptocing around with her. She always said what she thought.

But even she would be lost for words, I thought to myself, with what was happening to me now. I knew she would be upset that I hadn't called her on Thanksgiving, and that knowledge, that I was making her feel bad, made me sob even harder.

Because we came from Catholic child protective services and because my foster parents were God-fearing, I was sent to the local Catholic school, a fee-paying school.

It was the first time that St Francis Xavier's at 24th and Green was accepting blacks and Hispanics so I stood out like a sore thumb.

That first year was hard for me – I was used to being with my mom the whole time and wherever she was, that was the only place I ever wanted to be.

I'd put my hand up in class and ask to go to the bathroom then I'd walk home and ring the doorbell, fully expecting my mom to be happy I'd managed to navigate the long route back by myself.

'What are you doing here?' she'd scream, as I stood smiling on the porch.

'Momma, you miss me!' I'd insist. 'You need me to be home with you.'

It took me a little time to realize that every time I walked out of school and went back home, Mom took me straight back again, with a warning of a whooping if I pulled a stunt like that again.

The school was big – hundreds of pupils – yet there were only six black and Hispanic kids in the whole place. To this day I can still remember every single one of their names.

The white kids were suspicious at first and they didn't understand my racial background at all.

'You a black girl,' they'd tell me.

'Uh-uh,' I'd say, shaking my head. 'I'm Spanish – my birth mom is Mexican and my birth dad is Puerto Rican.'

'But your parents are black. I seen them!'

'Those are my foster parents,' I'd say wearily. I can't remember how many times I had to go through that whole routine.

'Well, whatever. Your mom is black and that makes you a nigger!' they'd jeer.

I'd want to punch their smug little faces – I think that's what they were trying to get me to do. But I'd always hold back. I didn't want to get into trouble. But I'd go home at nights, depressed, and report this new unhappy aspect of life to my mom.

She didn't have any time for my self-pity. 'This is just a part of life,' she'd say seriously. 'You gonna face this the whole of your life so if you don't get used to it now and change your way of thinking, you ain't never gonna get on.

'Don't feed into everything that everybody says, just because people are saying stuff. It don't matter what anybody else thinks or says. You are at school for one reason and one reason only – to get an education. That's your priority. You ignore the rest.

'And then, if you do need to fight, you get on the ground and you do this and that and get it over with.'

I giggled as Mom socked a punch to an imaginary opponent, but she wasn't joking around.

She looked at me hard. 'Josefina, suck it up! And if you can't do that, you fight and get it over with and move on. Got it?'

I nodded vigorously.

She thought I had to toughen up. And so I did. I got into a couple of fights, nothing serious, and within the first year I'd more or less learned how to stick up for myself.

If I ever whined or moaned about the girls in school, as all girls did, Mom would give me a severe talking-to. She didn't care what people said – as long as I got good grades.

'Why are you sitting round worrying about what everybody is saying when this is a C on your paper? It takes you three hours at night to do your homework because you're so worried about what everyone's saying. You need to adapt to the part of the program that you're there for, which is to get an education.'

Mom had to sign off on my homework every night.

One time she saw that I'd written a report and there was crossing out on one page where I'd made some mistakes.

'What's this?'

'I just had to change it. It's fine.'

'No, it's not fine. You do it over and do it right this time.'

It was a five-page report!

'I can just take this page out and replace it,' I argued.

'No. You got to learn how to do it right the first time. You're in such a rush to get it over with you're making all these mistakes. Take your time and pay attention to what you're doing and this won't continue to happen. Now, do it over.'

So I had to start my report over again from scratch. From then on I learned how to think about what I was doing, concentrate and do it right the first time.

Trust me, it did not happen too many more times because I was not going to keep continually doing my work over.

* * *

At first I got to see my birth brother Freddy and my birth sister Iris because we'd all been fostered by parents who belonged to the same Catholic War Veterans club. That's how my mom got the idea of fostering in the first place – another lady in the group had started fostering children. And once all Mom's kids were grown and she was in that big eight-bedroom house with just my dad she thought it might be nice to offer her home to a less fortunate child. She'd wanted a baby all along so when child protective services came up with me she was thrilled. I loved getting together with my brother and sister at the Catholic War Veterans club but on one occasion we were outside playing when Freddy grabbed me by the dress and it tore. It was an accident but the adults got all upset and said we couldn't see each other no more because we were 'abusive' to each other. It wasn't true.

I did pretty well at school, constantly getting As and Bs – only because my mom wouldn't accept anything else. Plus, I didn't find the work difficult. The school was strict though – if you stepped out of line you got your hand smacked with a ruler. I was a good all-rounder. I learned the saxophone and piano, I loved dancing – modern, jazz, tap and ballet. And I was even a cheerleader. I was popular too – other kids liked being around me.

The problem was, I got bored easily. I could learn stuff real quick and then I was always looking around for the next thing. And the next thing that came along was drugs. I guess I was no different to most teenagers in that I liked to experiment so I was thirteen when I started smoking weed. A lot of the kids in my area smoked and it didn't feel like a big deal. But I was always on the lookout for something more, something to get me higher. So I tried coke and it wasn't long before I was introduced to crack by some older kids.

I was hanging out at a friend's house one day when I saw her cooking up a rock of crack. And I was fascinated. I asked her if I could try some and she said sure.

Crack was unlike anything I'd ever tried before. On crack, I felt invincible and strong. That's what crack feels like, like you're capable of amazing things. So you can see why it's so addictive.

But I didn't think I was going to get addicted. I thought that I was just experimenting, I thought that I'd be able to try it, and then turn my back on it. I was just fourteen and at that age, you feel indestructible. Nobody tells you that if you start smoking crack you'll be an addict within a matter of months. And besides, where I lived, drug-taking was the norm. Yeah, there was a bit of peer pressure, and like most teenagers, especially when they're going through that stage where they're trying to gain independence from their parents, what my friends thought about me was more important than what my parents thought or said. Stretching boundaries is an important stage in everyone's development, but now I know that it's a dangerous one too, especially if you lived where I grew up, where drugs were everywhere and taking them was seen as a normal, everyday thing.

I got to admit, I felt like I had a lot of fun back then. I was just a regular teen and I liked to get high. The strange thing was that it didn't affect my studies. I was still getting home every night and going to school the next day. Still racking up the As and Bs and making all my extra courses.

Mom knew something was going on, of course she did,

but I was doing so well in school, doing all the things I was meant to do, that I guess she felt it couldn't be too bad.

I don't think she ever realized the true extent of my addiction or the pull of crack to take you so far off course you can never find your way back. Mom was strong, she was tough but in some ways she was completely ignorant. None of us knew back then how many lives and families would be ruined by the drug.

I saw whole streets fall victim: good families, good kids. But once they were hooked there was no going back. That's the way it was for me. And the deeper I went, the harder it became to remember what I wanted out of life. That's what addiction does – it takes everything from you until you want nothing else but to get high all the time, every day.

* * *

I wriggled the fingers on my left hand – they tingled and fizzed from going to sleep so long. I tried to do the same with my right hand but I could hardly feel it now. My back ached with being bent over for hours. The dampness seeped into my bones.

* * *

It wasn't long before I was selling drugs to make money to buy my own. They had a street corner at 18th and Wallace and I knew some people who had already been working for this group of dealers so I just joined in. I'd go and get four or five bundles of coke for as little as $10 a bag, sell them on for $25 and get my share out of the profits.

In the beginning we were getting $25 a bundle but the demand got so high eventually we had people sat in lines waiting to buy their bundles and we were making $50 a bag. It was mad money.

But then the dealers started to cut coke with other stuff to increase their profits, and that would set off my allergies, giving me rashes or making it hard to breathe. I was looking for an alternative source of income when my friend took me to a go-go bar. I was seventeen at the time and I remember looking up at these girls slinking and sliding all over the stage and thinking – wow, that's cute.

The lady who ran the place asked me if I wanted to give it a go. Sure, why not?

Since I'd danced all my life I knew I could do it and after I went in the first night I loved it. Best of all, the money was unreal – $400 a night in tips plus $10 a hour wages.

It really wasn't a great leap from go-go dancing to prostitution. After all, we were being propositioned in the bar every single night. That same year one guy asked me if I'd do something with him for $200. For $200 I was willing to give it a go. It was over in five minutes and for five minutes' work I earned hundreds of bucks. That sealed the deal for me. Most of the girls in the bar were hookers too – it was all just part of the same thing and with the drugs and the mad lifestyle I didn't see much wrong with it.

Mom didn't interfere either. Her neighbors might gossip at her. 'You know your daughter is out hooking,' they'd tell her after seeing me on the street.

'Yeah? Well, she can't be doing a real good job of it because she's spending all my money!'

Mom was never ashamed of me or judged me. She always thought that whatever I got into I would have to get out of myself. I had to learn my own lessons the hard way.

I was nineteen when I had my first child – LaToya. Her dad Billy and I had been together two years on and off. He took off when I fell pregnant and headed out to California, saying he had some friends there who could get him a job. I thought we'd be all set for a change of life and at seven months pregnant I followed him over to the West Coast. But when I got out there things weren't quite as Billy had led me to believe.

There was no job and no home – we were staying with some of his friends and I had no choice but to apply for welfare. As soon as my first check came through I bought a bus ticket home to Mom, just in time to give birth. Right from the start LaToya was a sweetheart – she wasn't a difficult baby and I loved being a mom. My mom babysat while I kept on going to school where I studied accounting.

I had plans, I had high hopes for myself but things never seemed to work out like I wanted them to. I never got back with Billy – while I was at college studying business management, I met Ronnie and we got married. Looking back I think I did it just to see what it was like. LaToya was three years old and I felt that she needed a father figure in her life – Ronnie was a great husband and a good provider. But, as always, I got bored real quick. After just a few months

I told him it wasn't working out for me – the routine of married life was too dull. I couldn't cope with doing the same things week in, week out. I was used to ripping and running. There were no hard feelings and we stayed friends but I moved out with LaToya and that's when I got mixed up with Robert.

He was trouble. He was the kind of guy who always wound up getting into fights. He'd have a few drinks then he'd start rowing with someone. Before long his friends would be pulling him away and he'd be walking off.

But then after just ten paces, Robert would turn around and shout at the guy: 'What did you say? What's that you saying about me?'

Yeah, Robert ended up in a lot of fights. But I loved him, of course.

By now I was heavily dependent on crack. I had to have a smoke of crack just to get going in the morning. I'd dropped out of the go-go club scene when I first got pregnant so now I was working the streets to get my customers. Since Robert was an addict too he didn't mind about the hooking. It was a whole different thing from picking up guys in the club but with my growing addiction, I didn't have much else I could do. I managed to stop when I fell pregnant with my second daughter Zornae, but after that, it all went wrong and I ended up back on the drugs.

I now had two children and crack had taken over my life completely. That's the thing about addiction – you don't know it's happening until it's too late and by then everything is such a mess you just keep going to forget how you've screwed everything up. So Ricky was born with drugs in his system – I'm not proud of that. The child protective services had taken his sister a few months before and they were threatening to keep him too. That's why he was in Pennsylvania Hospital, getting his weight up. LaToya was now five and she'd been with me until just six months previously when her dad Billy, now back from California after a year, had snatched her off me. Now he was making it difficult for me to even see her, let alone get her back again.

Luckily my mom still got to see Toya because Bill's mom would take her round for visits. She had seen Zornae a few times and was obviously cut up when she got taken but by this point my mom was more concerned about me and the drugs. She could see things weren't going well.

I'd split from Robert while I was pregnant with Ricky. I knew my lifestyle choices had screwed things up for my kids and me and I was determined to make things right again. I was tired of the drugs, tired of the streets and ready to get my kids back. It was time to change.

Two weeks before I'd appeared for a court hearing where the judge approved a social worker visit to inspect my new apartment at 6th and Gerard. I was determined to get all my kids back living with me. The new place I'd sorted out was a heated apartment and done up real good, and I felt motivated to start 1987 with a whole new attitude and life. I wanted to stop the drugs and I wanted to come off the streets. I was only going to keep smoking crack and working the streets until the kids came back, I'd told myself. Then everything will be different.

All of this was running through my mind as I was curled up in the hole. All of my bad decisions, the stupid risks I took, were torturing my mind as much as my restraints were torturing my body.

I knew I was taking a risk by going out on the streets that night but I never thought anything bad would happen to me. Yes, I'd had a lot of weird requests over the years, but most were pretty harmless. Some guys wanted you to do them with dildos, some liked to be chained up themselves, one guy liked me to put on high heels and walk over pastries! Then there were the ones who only wanted to talk and then paid you for your time, like you were a counselor.

Even the cops who occasionally picked me up liked me too much to charge me with anything. I'd even tricked for a few of them over the years so they didn't hassle me.

I was only twenty-five, but there wasn't a lot I hadn't seen, done or heard.

I never imagined I would be the one who'd get picked up by a guy who pulled a knife or worse.

I was too smart, too quick for that.

Now I was stuck in this hole and it was beyond anything I could have ever imagined. I thought of my mom again and I could hear her voice in my head: 'You're a fighter, Josie.'

A little sob escaped my lips – I didn't feel like a fighter. For the first time in many, many years I felt utterly, utterly helpless.

And stupid as hell.

Chapter Three

Gary

I couldn't think of anything else to do so I was still screaming and hollering, hoping someone would hear me, praying someone might come down and rescue me.

When my voice cracked with pain, I tried banging on the board over my head. I kept this up for ages until I heard vibrations of feet tramping overhead. He was down here. He was lifting the heavy earth-filled bags off the board, pulling the board aside and dragging me out of the hole by my hair.

'Argghhh!' I screamed in agony.

My vision was flooded with light and I had to squint against the harsh glare of the ceiling bulb.

Gary's huge form loomed over me – he was holding a long wooden stick. I saw him pull his arm back and then the stick came swooping through the air. I cowered in expectation of the pain to come, trying to shield my face with my quivering hands. And then – crunch!

The heavy pole came crashing down on my side, whacking all the air out of me and leaving me wheezing in shock.

Again, he raised the large stick in his hand and, gripping me by the hair, brought it down once again on my side. I was paralyzed with pain. Again and again the stick came down, now on my legs, back and buttocks.

I couldn't see him anymore through the pain and tears but his voice above me was unemotional and mechanical: 'Shut up. Shut up. Shut up.'

I was so disorientated and woozy from the beating that I didn't understand him at first and kept hollering, the blows thudding down so hard that every part of me was in torment. After a while my senses seemed to disconnect from my mind and I couldn't even tell where the stick was landing. *What am I doing?* I thought, *I don't need to shout. Nobody can hear me.*

I stopped screaming and he stopped beating me. I was crouched down with my head tucked into my body, but as the seconds ticked by without more beatings I dared to open my eyes and glance around me. This basement – it looked so different from just a day ago. When he put me in the hole I could have sworn I was at one side of the room, but it looked like I'd re-emerged in a totally different part of it. I was so confused and groggy I didn't even remember the layout of the room correctly.

I was starving, freezing and my throat was parched beyond belief, but these things hardly registered. My whole being was poised in anticipation of what he would do next. *Is this the moment he kills me?* I wondered. *How will it come?* I'd stopped panting, taking just small shallow breaths, ready for whatever came next.

As soon as Gary seemed satisfied that I wasn't going

to start hollering again, he forced me back into the hole. This time I wasn't down there more than thirty minutes before he was back in the basement, taking off the board and hauling me out again by my hair. He had a small cup of water in his hand and he gave it to me to sip. I got up enough strength to lift the polystyrene cup of water to my mouth and the water dribbled down my throat. It was instantly restorative – with that small trickle I could feel the strength returning to my body, my mind focusing back into the present. I took another sip – then another and another. I didn't want to gulp it all down too quickly as I knew it would make me sick.

He'd brought down a blue air mattress and he made me lie on it. Then he took down his trousers to have sex with me. I didn't struggle. I was too shattered and numb to even think to resist.

His grizzly beard stung at my face and grated against my cheek. Back and forth, back and forth, back and forth.

When he'd done he let out a satisfied sigh, then he pushed himself off me, swiveled his body so he was at right angles to me and laid his head on my lap. Then he fell asleep.

It was the most bizarrely intimate gesture in this whole violent encounter so far and I couldn't figure it out at all. I didn't know what this guy was going to do next and that made me even more scared.

I tried to stop myself from imagining the worst. Instead, I cast my eyes around the basement, looking for any means of escape. I saw his clothes – he'd not come back with the keys to the padlock for my chains so even if I could overpower him right now and knock him out, I would still be chained down here. I guess he'd kept the keys upstairs for exactly that reason – he was a nut all right but he wasn't stupid. The only thing I could see that gave me any cause for hope was a small air vent in the top of the wall opposite where I lay. I didn't know where it might lead but judging by the width, I reckoned I might be able to squeeze through.

He woke up with a start, unembarrassed by falling asleep in this way, and immediately got up to grab a spade that he'd brought down with him, digging the hole deeper and wider, filling up more plastic bags like the ones he'd placed on the board.

All the while he was talking.

'You know, Nicole, I brought you here for a reason,' he began, the cold steel of the shovel slicing through the damp, gritty earth. 'It's part of my plan. I want to have kids, you see. Lots of them. I got kids already but the state keeps taking them off me. Well, I got a way now of having kids so nobody can take them away anymore.

'You're just the start, Nicole. You gonna have my baby down here. But not just you – I want to get ten girls down here so you can all have my children and then I'll be able to raise my own kids without anybody interfering.

'You said you got kids so I know you can get pregnant – it's just going to be a matter of time.'

I didn't think I could feel any more scared but his words sent me shivering – I was here to have his babies? He intended to hold me captive down here for years, bringing another life into this nightmare world, and to bring more women down here too? It made me feel nauseous, with a sick creeping fear, especially when I thought about having a child here in this basement. It was obscene beyond belief and I was too dumbfounded to speak.

I knew he didn't want to kill me but it was little comfort to think that his plan was to keep me here for years to reproduce for him like a farmyard animal. Just the thought of having his child was enough to make me feel repulsed but knowing how he would keep and treat a baby born in this basement made my head swim.

How could he do that to a child – to *any* child – let alone his own?

Meanwhile, he rambled on: 'Damn child protective services keeps taking my children, interfering with my family life so that now I got to take matters into my own hands. The state takes one damn child after another off me and expects me to just sit there and take it, like an asshole? They owe me a family and one way or another I'm going to get one. After all this damn country has taken from me, it's the least I deserve.

'They took my mind first – hah! Took my damn mind and I didn't even know it.

'I was in the army. I worked as a medic in the army and I was real good too. Passed all my exams and did well – other fellas were jealous. I excelled above all of them. But did they give me the chance to work in the military police like I asked? Did they hell! Sent me to Germany as an orderly and that's where I got sick. Started having these pains in my stomach, dizzy spells, headaches and stuff. I went to the army doctors and they told me it was gastroenteritis. They start me on a load of drugs – I start seeing stuff, you know, visions and shit. I'm out for like three days and the next thing I know they've got me on some serious tranquilizers. That's where I reckon they tested all these mind-altering drugs on me. You heard of LSD?'

I nodded.

'That's what they tested on me. I went to the doctors with a medical complaint and by the time they'd finished treating me I was out of my fucking mind, doped up on Stelazine. That's some serious shit. Now I'm in and out of mental institutions because something has gone totally wrong with my brain and I didn't even realize until years later that they were the ones who did it to me! I was transferred back to Pennsylvania where they put me in a loony bin because I was seeing all this crazy shit that wasn't there. You know, like hallucinations. I didn't want to leave but after just a few weeks they gave me an honorable discharge on a disability pension. At first it was like just 10 per cent but they soon put it up to 100 per cent and backdated it from the date I left. So they must have done something to me there because they wouldn't have given me $2000 a month if it wasn't their fault in the first place.'

I was listening to his story, nodding my head as if I believed him. I was terrified, and confused, and I didn't know why he was telling me all this. Why did he feel the need?

'I know something's not right but the doctors, none of them are real clear about my diagnosis – they keep giving me labels like schizophrenic or schizoid personality, depressive, and so on, but nobody can agree on how to treat me and I've been on every kind of drug going because nothing seems to work right.

'There were plenty of times I knew I might do something bad so I'd put myself into the mental institution by telling them the type of stuff that gets their attention. I always knew what to say to get myself in and out of those places. Maybe I'd quit talking, or I'd swallow a load of rat poison. One time I got admitted by hitting my brother over the head with a wood plane. Those doctors, they think they're so damn smart. In the end, I was the one who was in control, not them. I always manage to make sure I get my disability payments, wherever I am.'

He talked and dug while I listened in silence – I felt the cold metal from the clamps cutting into my ankles as Gary continued to shovel earth from the hole, slowly, rhythmically, piling up the soil next to him into a crumbling pyramid. The more he talked, the more I could hear something underneath all the boasting and bragging, the bizarre life story. I hadn't quite got a hold of it yet, but I kept listening, trying to get a sense of what he was really saying.

'Anjeanette – she had my child. She was my girlfriend about ten years back and we lived at 2331 North 58th Street. Nice place, neighborhood like this one, but our place was okay. She wasn't too bright – I don't know, a lot of folks say she was retarded. Well, maybe she was. I can't say for sure. It didn't matter to me. She loved me and she would do anything for me. I think that made her happy – doing stuff for me like cleaning and cooking. She was completely happy being a housewife and liked to take good care of her man, you know? She loved me so much she would do anything I asked, including having kids. So when she got pregnant I was really pleased – I always really wanted kids but I'm scared, you know, cos she ain't too bright and child protective services don't like it when retarded women have children.'

I wasn't on best of terms with child protective services either, but I wondered whether it was more that they didn't want Anjeanette to have a child with this man, rather than worrying about her mental capacity.

'They wanted her to have an abortion – right from the off. These people who were meant to be looking out for her and helping her live her life you know, they just couldn't tolerate her being so happy with me and they plotted to try and get her to leave me. But Anjeanette wouldn't go. She'd tell me what they all said to her and how they conspired against my interests. And because I could tell that child protective services and her sisters were against me I stopped her going to hospital for her check-ups, cos I was afraid that one day she just wouldn't come back home. I'm a licensed nurse – I got my LPN certificate after leaving the army – and I knew I could treat her pregnancy at home instead of her getting all mixed up with the hospitals and all that. So that's what we were planning – she stays home and she's doing really well with me. But then her no-good fucking family start interfering and mess it all up.

'It's her damn sisters – interfering jealous little bitches. They didn't understand why Anjeanette had such a good life with this rich man who takes her out all the time to nice places and has not one but two Cadillacs in his garage. I know they're thinking – how come she gets it so good while we're all sitting round on welfare? And with her being retarded and all that. They were jealous, that was all. But Anjeanette did something that her sisters never did, she loved a white man. Her family didn't like that.'

Or perhaps they just didn't like you, I thought to myself.

'They take Anjeanette out of our home and admit her to the University of Pennsylvania hospital and now they're accusing me of all sorts of shit like starving her cos she's only gained five pounds the whole pregnancy. But that's just because she's so healthy. Anyway, they claim the baby could never have been born naturally because she had a tumor and they cut it out of her and took her away to foster her. What do you think of that bullshit?'

'Yeah, that sucks,' I murmured. I figured I had to play along for now. 'Maybe she's retarded but you're not. You could have looked after the baby.'

'Exactly! As the father, don't I have rights? And anyways Anjeanette wasn't too retarded to clean and feed the little girl. I got visitation rights to start with but they took those away too. These people, they don't let me have nothing of my own.'

'Yeah, sure,' I agreed. 'But you know, common sense will tell you if you want children you shouldn't be having them with retarded girls.'

'She wasn't that bad. Anyway, she loved me. She had a sister – Alberta. After they took the baby she was real upset and she wanted to go visit Alberta in this institution they'd had her locked up in since she was thirteen. Alberta wasn't much smarter than a four-year-old – couldn't count change or read or write. But she could feed and dress herself. She'd been locked up so long I took pity on her. I knew what it was like in them places. I told you, their family didn't give two shits about those girls. Alberta was just rotting away there – I took her out for the day with Anjeanette and we went for lunch. Like I said, I treated Anjeanette right – always took her out to eat and stuff. They were so happy to be together again. It was so touching to me to see Anjeanette happy after losing the baby so I wanted her to stay that way. Well, we take Alberta out shopping, buy her a dress and a new wig and she's really pleased to be with us. But when it comes time for Alberta to go back to that institution, the girls they don't want to be separated and they're weeping and sobbing all over each other, so much so it near breaks my heart.

'So we just don't take her back.

'I'm a nurse, like I said, and I saw they'd neglected her care because her hands are all sore – I started treating calluses on her hands and feet and trying to teach her about money.

'But the family and that damn institution where they've locked her up for twenty years goes crazy and they make it all out to be such a big deal. They come banging down my door and even though Anjeanette is begging me to hide Alberta so they don't find her, they track her down in the storage bin.'

This wasn't sounding good – he clearly had a history of abducting women. This was something he had done at least once before. I didn't like the sound of what he was telling me.

'And they take her away, claiming I'd abused her and abducted her, which I hadn't because I was only doing what she wanted and she was scared to go back to that place. She just wanted to stay with us.

'But the judge gets persuaded that I've kidnapped Alberta because they found her in my basement. I only told her to hide there because she didn't want them to find her. Now she couldn't take the stand because she don't know what the fuck's going on and all the felony charges like kidnapping, rape and false imprisonment, they have to drop all of those because they can't find enough evidence. Instead that damn judge gives me three to seven years for a load of bullshit misdemeanors like unlawful restraint, interfering with the custody of a committed person and one other, I forget what it is. My attorney can't believe the judge is being so harsh because I've got no prior convictions. Anyway, it don't make any difference. I get sent down and like I said, I know how to work the system, so instead of doing hard time I spend the next four years bouncing round the hospitals, tying all those doctors up in knots trying to figure out what's wrong with me.'

He broke out into a self-indulgent chuckle. 'I stop speaking for a while and I tell them it's because the devil has put a cookie down my throat. I just couldn't be bothered to be talking to no one at the time. I didn't have nothing to say. It didn't matter – it was all a game to me. I had to have ways to keep these guys guessing. They got me on Thorazine mostly now – I don't like it but they say I got to take it or I'll wind up back in the nuthouse.'

Gary had worked up a good sweat digging out the hole and he stopped for a moment, leaning on his spade to get his breath back.

'Them four years they stole from me though, they mattered, because when I got out I couldn't find Anjeanette. She just disappeared. So now I've lost a child and my girlfriend and all I've ever wanted is just to have family round me, my own family.

'But at least I've got money. I make sure that the army keeps up its disability payments to me every month. They owe me that and in the meantime you see I've managed to use that pension money to get into the stock market and I've turned that around for myself. So now I've built up a good amount of money and I'm not poor. That's how I can afford my cars – I've got a Rolls-Royce too.

'Then I get this white woman pregnant but she disappears with my son, Little Gary. So now I realize this isn't going well and I have to have another plan. I've seen that film – *The World of Suzie Wong.* You seen that film? I watch it and I think that maybe all those oriental women, they're far more accommodating to men, especially white men. So that's how I meet Betty – I sign up to this matrimonial bureau for oriental women and I see Betty's picture, beautiful girl. Stunning. We're writing pretty regularly to each other and then I propose because I think this is going to work. Betty comes over to the States from the Philippines and I do everything for her, and we get married.

'But it turns out she's not obedient like them Japanese and Chinese women – I didn't think I did the right thing by getting myself involved with a Filipino woman because she was always objecting to stuff. I tried to get her to adapt but she was very difficult. In the end she ran out on me when she was pregnant and now she's taken herself off and my son is out there somewhere but she won't let me see him, even though I supposedly still got to support the bitch.

'Turns out them Filipino women aren't so accommodating after all and now she's trying to bleed me through the courts but I'm fighting her all the way because if she thinks she can take my money and my son she's just plain out to lunch.'

I was just sitting there, listening to him rant on and on. *His* money, *his* son. It wasn't that he was sounding crazy to

me, he was sounding entitled. As if the world owed him for
what he had been through.

'That's the problem – that's been the problem all along,
Nicole. Everyone taking stuff from me, just takin' advantage
and never thinking it don't have no consequences.

'So, you see, that's how I came by this plan. This
way, nobody's going to leave and take my kids anywhere.
Eventually I'm going to move us all to the country – buy a
big house with lots of acreage and away from other people
so I can bring up my commune of kids in peace. That way
the kids can run around outside and play. Kids should be
outside, in the fresh air.'

I was too stunned to speak. And it was a good
thing too because if I'd recovered slightly I might have
shouted at him: 'Are you crazy? This is the dumbest idea
I've ever heard in my life and it will never, never in a million
years work!'

No, instead I just sat there and my silence spoke to him.
It told him I was compliant. It told him I understood his
plight, I understood what was going on.

This man was lacking very basic common sense. And
underneath all the madness, all the cunning and boasting
there was that sense of something he was reaching for,
something I could understand, something in him that I
could actually connect with.

Finally I spoke. 'You're lonely, aren't you?'

Gary turned and looked at me as if for the first time, as
if finally acknowledging the shivering, cowering woman he

had stolen from her life, now shackled and chained up in his basement.

He seemed surprised.

'I don't usually go for Hispanic girls,' he said after a while. 'I usually prefer black girls. And ones that aren't too smart, you know?

'That way they're not always nagging you the whole time and bitching at you. I picked you because you looked like Diana Ross.'

I almost laughed – the whole thing was so ridiculous.

'Maybe I made a mistake with you,' he went on. 'You're not dumb.'

Gary left to go upstairs again. This time he didn't put me back in the hole and he didn't put the handcuffs on either.

I sank to my knees and clasped my head in despair, letting my body rock forward so my head and hands met the ground. *Could this be real?* The whole thing seemed too crazy and far-fetched to be true. This man wasn't planning some sick torture for fun, he was serious, and it looked like his plan was set to last years, not days, weeks or months. *Years!*

Dear God, I prayed silently. *Please give me the strength to get out of here. Please give me the mental resilience to make it through this alive, to keep my wits about me and not let me falter.*

That night I prayed and prayed and prayed.

Chapter Four

Escape

I awoke on the floor, naked and freezing. Worse, I hadn't had anything to eat now for nearly two days.

These, however, seemed like the least of my worries. Now I knew what fate Gary had in mind for me, I knew that somehow I had to get out of here. There was no way on earth I wanted to become part of his sick baby-making harem.

The guy was obviously out of his mind. What if he decided it wasn't such a good plan after all? He couldn't just let me go – he'd have to get rid of me somehow and I knew he wouldn't let me walk out of here. Overhead somewhere I heard the front door slam and felt the vibrations as he revved up his Cadillac in the garage. I listened intently as the car slowly rolled away. Now was my chance.

I shook the fuzzy, cloudy feeling from my head and started to look around. There weren't any windows in the basement. The whole room was set underground and cemented from wall to wall.

I wandered round and round the basement, pulling my heavy chain behind me, examining every part of each wall – luckily, the chain was long enough for me to reach all parts of the basement so inside that room, I was more or less free to move around.

The only part of the room that didn't seem to be made of cement was this little hole at the top of the far wall with a small door on it.

I walked over to the wall and I put my face against the door – I could feel a breeze coming out of it so I knew it must lead to the outside. For the first time since I got down here I had hope.

Quickly I squatted down on the ground and fiddled with the clamps around my ankles. The left side was completely stuck but there was a tiny bit of give in the screw on the right clamp. In the last few days I'd been fiddling with this screw, running my fingernail along the edges of the dried glue to pick it off. After working on this for days, most of the glue had flaked off and now I set to work again, digging and picking at it like mad. After half an hour the rest of it came away and I could start undoing the screw. It was tough but eventually it spun under my fingers and before long I had one free foot, my ankles red and sore from where the clamps had dug into the skin.

I tried again with the left clamp but it was no good and I figured if I wasted any more time trying to get it off then he'd come back and catch me. With one foot free I had at least a little bit of maneuverability and I decided I had to try to get out one way or another.

The little metal door that formed the entrance of the hole easily came away in my hands. I could see the space inside was around a foot and a half wide, just enough for me to crawl through. So I got inside and dragged myself along, trying to get out as far as possible. I was outside now – I knew because I could feel the wind on my face and it was broad daylight. The yard was littered with trash and I could hear voices coming from the front of the house.

I wriggled as far as possible so that most of my body was out of the hole, except my left leg, which was still attached to the chain inside, and I started yelling for my life.

'Help! Help! Please help me! This guy's got me chained up in his basement and he's raping me. Somebody get me out of here.'

I paused, waiting for someone to answer me, for someone to come and help. But all I heard was the low murmur of those voices standing out the front of the houses.

I tried again. 'Please come and help me. I'm in the basement of this guy Gary's house. He's got me locked up down here. Someone please call the police. Someone please help me. Please help me.'

Still, no response, so I switched to schoolgirl Spanish.

'*Por favor, venga y me ayude. Estoy en el sótano de la casa de este hombre Gary. Me tiene encerrado aquí abajo. Alguien por favor llame a la policía. Alguien por favor me ayude. Por favor, ayúdame.*'

I was out there, lying on the ground and I was yelling and yelling, hoping and praying someone, *anyone* would answer me. They had to be able to hear me. I could hear *them*! Loud and clear.

I grabbed the only thing within reaching distance – a wooden stick – and started beating the fence dividing Gary's yard from the neighbor's yard. I beat on that fence and kept right on screaming and I was beating so hard that the whole fence was starting to come down.

I must have been out there for twenty minutes, screaming myself hoarse, but no one took any notice and the next thing I knew, I felt a yank on my chain.

Gary was back – he'd got hold of the chain inside and he was trying to pull me back in, reeling me in like a fish on the line. But I wasn't giving in that easily. I resisted with every bit of strength I had left in me, wedging my free foot against the opening to the hole so that he couldn't get my body back through to his basement. There was nothing to hold onto outside so I just put my arms down flat and pushed my torso off the ground so I was in the strongest position possible. He was pulling and pulling and I was still screaming, desperate now, desperate for someone to come to my rescue.

'Please, will someone please just call the cops. He's crazy – he's chained me up. Please help. I know you can hear me. Just call the cops. Call the goddamn cops! This nut is gonna kill me – please help! HELP!!'

I felt the chain relax on my leg and I knew that he'd left the basement. Still I was screaming and nobody was responding.

And there he was. Gary came into the yard and towered over me, a stony-eyed look of fury on his face.

Without saying a word, he tried pushing me back into the hole but I fought him and he couldn't get a hold on my limbs to push them back in. We were scuffling in his backyard, a naked woman on the ground with one leg chained inside the house. It was broad daylight, and still nobody responded.

I was shrieking now: 'Get off me! Let go, you bastard! GET OFF!'

After five minutes of this he gave up and returned to the house. I didn't know what else I could do except keep right on shouting. I still had hope that somebody would hear me and call the cops or do something.

OH SHIT!

I felt a jolt up my leg as if someone had just tried to rip it right out of its socket. Gary was tugging on the chain with all his might. This time there was no messing around. The force on my leg was so immense I felt it might break.

He gave the chain another yank and I realized with gut-wrenching clarity that unless I let go right now he was going to break one or both of my legs.

I relaxed my free leg and let it slide next to the one inside the hole just in time for another heft so strong that it nearly pulled me through in one go.

There was nothing I could do as I felt myself slide back down onto the basement floor. His force was so great I could tell he would have broken every bone in my body before letting me get free.

Now he set to work again, redoing the clamp on my leg and setting it with the Krazy Glue again.

All the while he was talking to me, almost in amazement.

'I can't believe you got out there!' he said, as if the very idea of there being a hole in his plan, or his basement for that matter, never even occurred to him.

'Jeez, you were out there hollering and screaming for ages. But you know why nobody responded? It's because they're all the drug guys and I help them out and give them money and stuff so they like me, they leave me alone. That's why they ignored you and didn't pay you any attention.'

He was working and talking quickly, high on the adrenaline from the drama and the effort, excited by his victory.

Now he was redoing the other clamp too, just to be sure neither of them came off again. I felt utterly despondent. I had one chance and it failed.

I couldn't believe in all that time nobody responded. Nobody called the police. If I heard a girl screaming 'Help! Help! Help!' at the very least I'd pick up the phone to the police and say: 'Hey, something's going on, somebody's screaming and hollering for their life.' I wouldn't just ignore them! Shame on those people. The tears began to well up behind my eyelids again.

I hardly noticed as Gary pulled my arms behind me and put the cuffs on again. And I hardly felt the blows as he took up his wooden stick and started to beat me, dull thumps landing all over my body.

'Try something like this again,' he grunted. 'And not only will you fail, but I'll kill you.'

I didn't doubt him for a minute.

Gary tramped back upstairs, leaving me lying there on the floor, my body covered with fresh bruises from his beatings and my hands cuffed behind me. I was so exhausted all I wanted to do was sleep but if I thought sleeping was hard enough in the hole or with the chains on, sleeping in the cuffs was impossible. There was no way to get comfortable. I tried rolling onto my front but my head was forced to the side and I could barely breathe for the pressure on my chest.

So I rolled onto my side but soon the arm I was lying on began to ache and then it went to sleep. Eventually I tried leaning my back against the wall, my legs bent slightly to support myself, and let myself fall forward so my head rested on my knees.

* * *

Time moved in strange ways now – I couldn't tell how long it had been since I'd been like this. All hope had left me. I was too exhausted and wrung out to even think straight. I guess my body was probably suffering from drug withdrawal too, but I didn't think about crack once.

Finally, Gary returned and this time he brought down some bread and water. He uncuffed my arms and they just flopped down uselessly by my sides. I couldn't even lift them up – my brain was telling my arms to move but they refused.

I took a tiny sip of the water – it felt amazing, instantly bringing me round from my woozy state. Then I picked up one of the two slices of white bread Gary had put down next me and tentatively, scared almost of what it might do,

I took a bite. Until that moment I'd hardly thought of food at all – I'd missed several meals but nothing could have been further from my mind. It just hadn't occurred to me that I needed to eat. Aside from anything else, my lips were cracked and swollen and my tongue seemed too big to fit in my mouth properly.

At first, my jaws were stiff, like they'd rusted up from lack of use. I tasted the floury, sweet bread and let it sit in my mouth awhile, accustoming myself to the sensation of food again. Then I worked the morsel round my mouth, chewing and breaking it up into smaller and smaller pieces until it was small enough to go down into my stomach. My throat must have closed up some because it felt like I had to work that bread for ages before I could get it down.

But the effect, like the water, was instant. As soon as the food reached my stomach I felt a yawing hunger scream out from inside me. I'd been starved and now my body needed food like nothing else. I took another bite, working this piece quicker, getting it down easier than the first, and slurping a quick drink of water to help it down.

All the while Gary had gone back to digging the hole, carrying on like nothing was unusual, like this was just a regular day for him. I didn't have hope that anybody would come – I knew that if there was going to be a visit from the cops, it would have happened by now. All I knew was that there wasn't any crawl space in the wall anymore. Gary had filled it in with white plastic bags and bolted the metal door to the wall.

After he finished his digging, Gary laid me back down on the air mattress and had sex with me. He pulled down his jeans, shifted his large long body over mine and then just began pumping up and down, his mouth set in a fixed line the whole time. His tousled brown hair bobbed up and down, his heavy torso pounded on top of me and I could smell his sour breath, like old coffee. I turned my head away. When he was done, he rolled off, reattached the handcuffs and returned upstairs.

I began to despair, wondering if I would ever get out of this place alive. I drifted off to sleep without realizing then awoke, thinking I was still asleep.

This is all just a dream, I told myself drowsily. *I'll wake up soon in my own bed and then I can go back to the hospital, see my little Ricky and call my mom.*

I lapsed into unconsciousness again but I never woke up in my own bed. Every time I opened my eyes, I was still in that basement, my arms pinned behind my back, the clamps digging welts around my ankles, the harsh glare of the overhead bulb punishing my sight while the radio blared monotonously on and on in the background. I was locked into a frightening new reality, one that seemed further and further from the one I used to know.

* * *

Gary returned some hours later for another round of bread and water. He had sex with me and afterwards he put me in the hole. It was bigger now and before he put me down there, he crammed the air mattress in. Now I was in the hole and I wasn't crumpled up any longer – there was enough space for me to sit up with my arms and legs in a normal relaxed position. It felt comparatively luxurious.

Shortly after that I realized he had put me in the hole because he was leaving the house. I knew this because a few minutes later I felt a strange vibration through the ground and the unmistakable roar of his Cadillac. He was moving his car out of the garage.

I started to panic.

Gary leaving the house was scarier than him being in the room. What if something happened to him while he was out there? What if he got knocked down and killed or arrested and locked up? Nobody knew I was here. I'd just rot away and this hole really would be my grave.

Every time he walked back upstairs I knew it could be the end. But now that I had a little food and water, I felt my mental strength return and my desire to live kicked in with full force.

I wanted to see my kids again – I wanted to see my mom, to have her put her arms around me and tell me everything was going to be okay. I wanted to build a better future for myself, give my kids a chance at a good life. This wasn't how it was going to end, not like this.

I knew I had to get out of this and I was going out the same way I came in – walking through the front door. *Nobody's gonna take me out of this hellhole in a body bag!*

My first attempt to escape had failed but that didn't mean I wouldn't succeed at some point.

I just had to be smarter about this, work out a way so that the next time I tried to leave, I did it right. Of course, I didn't know how on earth I was going to achieve this – right now, I was completely stuck.

But if I just waited, I told myself, something would turn up.

Just hang on. Hang on, Josefina, and don't give up the fight.

Chapter Five
Sandra

I heard the girl before I saw her.

I was in the hole and I could hear sobbing coming from upstairs and two sets of footsteps padding down the basement steps.

Then I heard Gary hollering, 'Shut up, Sandra! You know you know me. You know I'm not going to hurt you. Just shut up – why are you crying?'

The footsteps got closer and closer until they were right over the top of me – the bags were removed, the board slid away and Gary pulled me out of the hole by the arm.

He was holding a naked black girl with his other arm; her hands were cuffed behind her back, just like mine were when he first brought me down here, and she was weeping uncontrollably.

'Sandra, Nicole. Nicole – this is Sandra,' he said, as if introducing a pair of strangers at a dinner party. I looked at the poor girl, naked and shivering, obviously confused and scared as hell. Just like I when he had brought me here, three days ago by my calculations.

Round, frightened eyes peeped out from behind large, thick-lensed glasses.

'I don't know why Sandra here is crying.' Gary went on, now taking a new pair of muffler clamps and attaching them to her ankles, just like he did with me. 'I know Sandra. She's been in my house many times. She knows I'm not going to hurt her.'

But Sandra just wouldn't quit sobbing and my heart went out to her. Snot dribbled down her nose, she was gasping now, taking big gulps of air. I could see why she might be distressed – after all, if she'd been here before I'm sure she was wondering why he was chaining her up this time instead of letting her out the door as usual. *This can't be good*, I thought. *This can't be good at all*. Now he was taking women he knew.

Gary went through the same routine with the clamps as he did with me – screwing them on, applying Krazy Glue then drying them with the hairdryer. The sheer strangeness of the process was enough to stop Sandra crying. She looked like she couldn't quite believe what was happening. It struck me that until this moment I hadn't imagined Gary taking any more girls. He'd told me of his plan but the whole thing seemed so crazy, so unbelievable, I guess I hadn't imagined it would ever happen.

Now here he was, bringing down another girl and I realized with sickening clarity that the baby farm had begun in earnest.

Gary attached Sandra's chains to the same water pipe with a padlock, undid her handcuffs and put us both in the hole together.

He slid the board back over, replaced the bags on top and went back upstairs.

'Are you okay?' I asked.

'Yeah, I think so,' she sniffed. I couldn't see her any longer but I could feel her thighs next to mine as we lay side by side on the air mattress in the dark. Now we were two naked women, complete strangers, lying side-by-side in little more than a shallow grave. It was crazy, weird and extremely frightening.

'I don't understand it. Gary's my friend – why's he doing this? I been here a ton of times.'

Sandra talked slowly, I could tell she wasn't all that bright – *just Gary's type*, I thought – but she was sweet. She knew something had gone horribly wrong in her life.

'What happened?' I asked.

'We been friends a long time. He's always been so nice, takes me out to eat and stuff. We met at Elwyn Institute and we've been friends ever since.'

'Elwyn – what's that?'

'It's a place for mentally handicapped folks – he's there a lot. Anyways, we get to talking one day and it goes from there. We been friends a few years now.

'He picked me up today and took me to McDonald's like normal. Then we came back here to have sex but afterwards he started strangling me and that's when he brought me downstairs.'

'That's the same thing that happened to me too,' I said. Now Sandra was over her crying fit, she seemed quite well recovered. There was something about the way she was talking, like she couldn't quite believe Gary, her friend Gary, could possibly do anything to harm her.

I wondered now if my being here had helped calm Sandra down – after all, when I arrived there was no one here at all, nobody to reassure me and say 'It's okay, he doesn't want to kill you'. Sandra had regained her composure in a matter of moments. Now she was talking fluently and without erupting into tears.

I wanted to know more about this Gary she knew, the one who was nice and took her out to eat. The more I knew about him, the better chance I had of getting out.

'He's got a church,' she said. 'It's called the United Church of the Ministers of God and he holds his sermons here, in his house, and lots of us folk that like Gary and feel he understands us, we come and he teaches us hymns and reads to us from the Bible. He's always real kind – afterwards he usually takes us all out for lunch to McDonald's or Roy Rogers. He never collects any money from us – his church don't have a collection plate, which is good, because a lot of us can't afford to give away none anyway.'

'A church?' I repeated. 'Here – in this house?'

It seemed so unlikely. How was this apparently soft, generous God-fearing man related to the monster who locked up women in his basement to bear his children?

It didn't add up.

'What's going on with all of this?' Sandra asked me.

She seemed so innocent, so naïve. I felt very protective towards her.

'He's got a plan,' I told her. 'He wants to get ten women down here, all chained up, and he wants us all to get pregnant with his babies and then he's going to bring up all the children down here, in the basement in secret, so nobody can take them away.'

'Hmm, he's been wanting babies for some time,' said Sandra. 'Child protective services kept taking them and it always really upset him. He had a mail-order bride and they had a kid together but she ended up leaving him.

'She used to come to his church before she left but she wouldn't like to pray so he'd make her stand in a corner on her own. You know, I think he was trying to teach her a lesson but she didn't want nothing to do with the church and she ran away.'

Sandra paused. I could feel that she was starting to shiver – whether from the shock or the cold I couldn't tell. I tried to be positive.

'Look, Sandra, we're going to get out of here. I don't know how this is going to work yet but I'm going to think of something. Don't worry.'

At some point we must have both fallen asleep because the next thing we knew, Gary was pulling the board off and yanking us up from the hole in order to have sex with us. He lay us both down on the air mattress side by side and had sex with first me, then Sandra.

There didn't seem to be any pleasure or passion in it – it was straightforward sex, up and down, mechanical like a chore. And we both submitted. What would be the point of resisting?

I tried to switch off from what he was doing and concentrate instead on the radio – they were playing 'Smooth Operator' by Sade.

I sang along to the song in my head, ignoring what was happening to my body.

When he was done he showed us he'd brought down a portable loo so we could use the bathroom when we needed to, which was an improvement on the bucket I'd had to use previously, and he gave us each a shirt to put on. It was the first time I had worn a stitch of clothing in three days and I felt stupidly grateful. It was the middle of winter and in the unheated basement, the cold was relentless, unforgiving.

Then he picked up the spade and started digging out the hole again. Sandra and I just sat there in silence, watching him.

* * *

Our lives now settled into a strange new routine. First thing in the morning Gary would bring down a couple of slices of bread each and some water. He would then have sex with us and afterwards, while he was digging, we just sat there in the basement. He'd brought down a battery-powered black and white TV so when he put us back in the hole afterwards, he placed the TV down in there with us so we could watch TV for a couple of hours. That was all the batteries could last for until they ran out of power.

One time, we were sat watching *Wheel of Fortune* when suddenly I sensed the air around me thicken and my breathing became heavy and difficult.

'You all right?' I whispered to Sandra.

'No,' she said. 'I can't breathe.'

'Me neither.'

The air around us seemed to be seeping out of the hole, like something was sucking the oxygen out of there. In a few moments we were both gasping for breath.

So we started banging on the board and screaming but of course the music was still blaring throughout the house so Gary couldn't hear us.

Now, I was panicking. My head became light, I felt dizzy. I didn't want to die down here! I couldn't believe that I wouldn't see my children again, not tell my mom I loved her. I couldn't allow that to happen.

'Here, come on!' I urged Sandra as I tried sliding my arms underneath the heavy, weighted-down board in order to try and get some air in the hole. We managed to both wriggle our forearms underneath the board, just enough to let in some fresh air. It was such a relief. Instantly my head cleared and the cool air allowed us to take in big lungfuls of oxygen. We stayed that way, our bodies angled awkwardly to allow the air to rush in, for about half an hour until we heard Gary's footsteps. Then we quickly pulled our arms back in but the board was so heavy it scraped along our arms, leaving us both with scorched bleeding scrapes.

'Hey,' he said as he pulled us both out of the hole. 'What's up with your arms?'

'We had to put them under the board,' I told him. 'To let some air into the hole. We ran out of air to breathe.'

'Hmmm, I wonder why that could be.' Gary looked thoughtful. Then he spied the TV still on in the hole. 'It's that thing,' he said, pointing to it. 'It must be the batteries, sucking all the oxygen out of the hole. You girls got to learn how to limit your time with that thing otherwise you're gonna suffocate yourselves. And you better keep those cuts clean because if they get infected and I can't treat them, you're gonna be in trouble. Nobody's going to hospital.'

So we learned to eke out our precious two hours of TV over the whole day. We switched on for a sitcom that Sandra liked called *Amen*. It was set in a church near to where she grew up so that's why she liked it. She found it real funny but I gotta say, it didn't do much for me. It was a distraction, nothing more. Just something to take my mind somewhere other than that hole. We didn't watch anything serious or depressing. We didn't even watch the news – it was hard to think of the world outside, a world where everything was normal. If people were looking for us I just hoped they found us quickly and if they weren't looking for us, I didn't want to know. So we only tried to watch happy, upbeat stuff – sitcoms, game shows, panel shows. I didn't even like seeing the weather channel. What was the point?

I was thinking about my kids a lot too – LaToya, Zornae and Ricky. I had only been with Ricky for such a short amount of time, but I had memorized everything about him – his little fingers, the whorls of dark hair on his head, his little rosebud lips. I was thinking about Zornae and her shy but winning ways, such personality, even for a toddler. I imagined they had probably been taken in by a foster family and hoped that whoever they were with, they were taking good care of them both. And Toya, of course, my funny cheeky girl, now with her father. Thinking about my kids gave me hope and a reason for getting out of there.

Several times a day Gary came down to dig out the hole or have sex with us.

In between Sandra and I slept or talked. She told me she lived with her mom and sisters and liked to go to Bible study or walk in the park. It seemed she lived a simple, uncomplicated life, grateful for the few friends she did have. I told her about my kids and my mom. When we got tired of talking we just lay in silence.

Late in the evening Gary would bring down two more slices of bread and some more water. He also brought down a small portable coffee pot, some tea bags and sugar so we could make sweet tea when we were out of the hole. We rationed our tea bags so we had no more than two a day but we packed each Styrofoam cup with about ten spoons of sugar to try to fill ourselves up and stave off the hunger pangs.

The radios were still blaring throughout the house but after a few days me and Sandra begged Gary to change the channel because we'd realized that on this station they just played the same ten songs over and over again, every twenty minutes. I'd heard that damn Anita Baker song so many times now, it'd driven me half mad. It was like torture. I never realized up till now that the stations all had certain tracks that they played over and over again. I couldn't even bear to listen to the same radio presenters anymore. Their chirpy, upbeat banter was so fake, so forced. At least, it seemed that way to me.

Whenever Gary left the house he put Sandra and me back in the hole – otherwise he seemed happy to leave us in the basement in our chains. I hated it when we had to go back in the hole again – there was more room now but every time I climbed in and I heard his footsteps on the front porch and felt the vibrations of his Cadillac, I feared he was never coming back.

After a few days, Sandra relaxed – she didn't stress about whether she was going to live or die. But I was wound up pretty tight most of the time. Every time we were on our own, I grilled her about Gary. She filled me in on how he'd been through a lot of bad episodes in his life, tried to kill himself a number of times.

She even went to visit him in hospital after one occasion. Apparently he was supposed to take Thorazine every day but he didn't like to take it and sometimes he hoarded it so that he could take a killer dose when he was feeling suicidal.

The medication thing was something that stressed me out a lot. How can you relax when you're at the mercy of a madman? I studied Gary now, trying to pick up on any little detail that might help me get out of here. Sometimes I could tell when he hadn't taken his medication. His movements were jerky, his eyes darted about wildly and he seemed jittery, on edge.

Those nights I stayed awake, gripped by fear.

I imagined him tormented by evil thoughts, his mind plagued by voices telling him to get rid of the girls in the cellar.

'What do we do if he comes down and he wants to get rid of us?' I voiced my fears to Sandra.

'We'll just have to try and hurt him first,' she said, in her usual slow, deliberate manner.

'Yes but he doesn't bring the keys down here with him. So if we hurt him or killed him even, we'd still be trapped down here. No, we got to try and talk him out of it. How do we do that?'

'I don't know.'

'You ever seen him when he's like, you know, really out of it?'

'I'm not sure. But you know, Gary, he don't like to be told "no" all that much. He sure didn't appreciate it when his wife said no to him – she got punished a lot for that.'

'Yeah, I get that.' My mind was racing on, unable to stay still for even a second. 'So we have to tell him the plan is working, that he needs to stick with the original idea of getting us all knocked up. Try to keep him on course. We could say that we were pregnant!'

'That's a good idea, Nicole. But how do you prove it to him?'

'I've been pregnant before so I'll just say that I know the feeling and you know, when a woman knows she knows.'

Sandra was silent. I couldn't tell if she was falling asleep. Was it late? I had no idea. Still my mind kept turning over all the different possibilities. Whatever happened next, I wanted to be prepared. Everything was so out of control, I had to get hold of something.

My one crumb of comfort was Sandra's insight into Gary and the man she described on the outside was like a different person altogether – a soft, kind man.

It gave me some kind of hope that there was another Gary outside of this basement, a Gary with a heart.

If he had a softer side that meant he could feel kindly towards people, I reasoned. He wasn't just this cold and calculating baby-obsessed freak, he had humane characteristics. And all these people he was gathering round him at his church, these unfortunates, the outcasts of society, the mentally and physically handicapped like Sandra described who attended his services, these were his folk. He surrounded himself with these types of people because it made him feel good, like King Gary. These people were all those who looked up to him, who accepted him as a man and a person in society.

This was what he needed to make himself feel normal.

All the really normal folk in his life – the doctors, child protective services, and the people of the state – these were the ones who seemed like they were against him.

* * *

The days drifted by, no different from the nights. When we heard a song we liked on the radio we'd hum or sing along – we both loved Prince and occasionally we heard 'When Doves Cry', one of my favorites. Otherwise, we tried to block out the constant noise that thrummed through the cellar.

Sandra told me about the simple life she'd led so far, getting no more than a high-school diploma through a special education program. She'd lived at home all her life with her mom, protected by her loving sister Tess and her cousins.

We were the same age, twenty-five, though it felt like Sandra was still a child – a trusting, kind, young girl.

She had something wrong with her jaw – the upper and lower part didn't quite meet when she ate so it took her a long time to chew and swallow her food.

Each meal could take up to an hour for her to consume because she spent such a long time chewing her food over and over, slowly, like a cow chewing its cud.

A few days after Sandra first arrived, when Gary was down with us in the basement there was a banging on the door upstairs. We were all surprised – in the whole time I'd been here nobody had knocked. Gary didn't get visitors. But this person wasn't just knocking, they were banging away for minutes. Gary kept right on digging out the hole, breaking the earth with slow heavy movements. I think he was hoping that the person would just give up and go away. But whoever it was out there, they weren't going anywhere in a hurry. After twenty minutes of this, Gary sighed, threw down the spade, put Sandra and me back in the hole and went upstairs. We couldn't hear what was going on because the radios were on but we heard the banging go on for another ten minutes until eventually it stopped.

Gary returned a few minutes later and let us out of the hole.

'Just my neighbors,' he said casually.

At the time we accepted that – we didn't have any reason to believe any different. But now I know this was a lie. The people at the door weren't Gary's neighbors – it was Sandra's sister Tess and her two cousins. Within hours of Sandra going missing her family had tried to track her down. They knew that Sandra was friends with Gary and they also knew, through Sandra and Gary's mutual friend Tony Brown, another of Gary's church followers, that the last anyone had heard of Sandra, she was heading over to Gary's house.

Sandra's mother had reported her missing to the police.

An officer, Sergeant Armstrong, visited North Marshall Street, and like Sandra's relatives, he got no answer when he knocked.

Armstrong managed to track down Tony Brown to try and get more information about Gary.

When he asked him how to spell his surname Tony said: 'H-E-I-D-A-I-K-E.'

So Armstrong returned to his computers and looked up the wrong name and found nothing. A perfect opportunity to stop Heidnik in his tracks was missed and all thanks to the wrong spelling of a name.

Had Armstrong looked harder, maybe tried different spellings, he would have found out a whole lot of worrying stuff about Gary Heidnik. Like his history of locking up retarded black girls in his basement.

And his mental condition.

As it was, the visits only served to alert Gary to the fact that her family was on his trail. And that set him thinking.

Chapter Six

Screwdriver

The next evening Gary came down wearing a pair of leather gloves and holding a piece of paper, an envelope and a pen. He put the pen and paper on the table where he'd set up the coffee pot and tea and got Sandra to sit down.

'Here, you take this pen,' he ordered. She did as she was told.

'Now, just write what I tell you. Nothing else. Just my words. Do it wrong and we'll start again. Do you understand?'

'Yes Gary.' Sandra nodded obediently.

'Okay – now write this: DEAR MOM.'

Sandra crouched down close to her writing hand and with extreme concentration, she carved out the letters on the page.

Gary looked at her handiwork – it was the scrawl of an elementary school kid but he had clearly seen her writing before because he seemed pleased with her efforts.

'Good. Okay next, write: I AM FINE.'

Again, Sandra bent down close to her hand to etch the words.

In the end, the letter he made her write went like this:

'Dear Mom. I am fine. I am in New York and I'll get in touch with you soon. Don't worry. Love Sandra.'

Then Gary made her handle the letter real good so she got her fingerprints all over it and finally he made her write her mom's name and home address on an envelope.

We both knew what this meant. Gary was trying to throw Sandra's relatives off the scent. After he'd given us a couple of slices of bread each he put us in the hole and we listened as his car left the garage.

We were expecting him to be back in a few hours as usual but we were waiting the whole night long and we never heard him come back.

This set my nerves off again – what if he'd got into an accident?

'It'll be fine,' said Sandra drowsily. 'Don't worry none. Just try and get some sleep.'

I tried but my mind was racing all night long and my senses were on edge, just waiting to feel that familiar rumble in the ground that signaled his car was back in the garage. It never came.

The next day we didn't see Gary at all and I was wretched with worry, so by the time his car pulled into the garage that evening, over twenty-four hours since he'd put us down there, we were so relieved and so happy to see him that we were babbling over one another, hardly knowing what we were saying, not realizing our words were giving him cause for concern.

'Thank God you're back,' I exclaimed as he pulled me out

of the hole. 'We didn't know whether you were ever coming back. Then when we heard your car pull in the garage we were so relieved. We were so happy because, you know, we figured maybe you'd got into an accident or something.'

Gary stopped and looked at me hard as I was saying this.

'How did you hear my car?' he asked. For the first time I realized he didn't know that we could hear him coming and going when we were in the hole.

He'd gone to a lot of trouble to make sure the radios were on all the time so we couldn't hear what was going on upstairs and nobody outside could hear us either.

And it was true, if you were in the basement above ground then you couldn't normally hear a thing because the radios drowned out any other sound.

But in the hole, we were under the ground, where the radio waves didn't travel and we could pick up the vibrations from heavy movements around us.

Sandra filled him in, unable to sense his shift in mood: 'We can hear the car from the hole.'

Gary put down some bread and water next to us then he went back upstairs. Sandra was still relieved, happy even, that Gary was back.

'See, I told you it'll be all right,' she said. 'He came back.'

But now I had a feeling something bad was coming. I could sense Gary wasn't happy with us being able to hear him.

Later, we learned the reason for the 24-hour absence – he'd driven all the way to New York from Philly to post Sandra's letter and that's why he was away for a whole day.

And it worked too – when Sandra's relatives got the letter, they presented it to Armstrong, who immediately dismissed their concerns for her safety, assuming it was just another case of a runaway girl.

But back then, we were in complete ignorance. I wondered if he had another girl stashed upstairs.

No, when he came back down, it wasn't with a woman, but a handful of screwdrivers.

And then, like a man with a DIY task to complete, he set to work.

First he got Sandra and he pushed her down on the ground so he could turn her head to the side.

'Now don't you go screaming when I do this,' he warned her. My heart was in my mouth. What was he going to do?

Straddling her, he took one of the screwdrivers and deliberately pointed it into her ear and started pushing it in, hard.

'Agghhh!!' she screamed in agony.

My mouth fell open in horror, a silent cry hanging in the air.

'STOP IT!' Gary shouted at her. 'Stop screaming – just let me do this. Don't worry – you know that I'm a licensed nurse, I know just how far I can push it in without making you deaf. I just want to deaden your eardrums a little so you can't hear me coming and going.'

But Sandra couldn't help herself – she was letting out pitiful strangled little shrieks as the pain seared into her ear. Now there was blood pouring out and Gary sat back, seemingly happy with his handiwork.

Slowly, he turned her over so now her bleeding ear was resting on the ground and he repeated the same torture on her other eardrum.

I was so shocked I couldn't do anything except shake with fear, knowing it was my turn next. And soon enough Gary pushed me down onto the ground and he had the full weight of his body on top of me while my ear was pointed at the ceiling, exposed and ready for him to drill into.

I smelled the rich earthiness of the ground next to me, my cheek now squashed against the hard soil. I started to sob with fear.

The pain when it came was so severe, it made me dry heave. I thought I was going to pass out as he pushed down harder and harder, twisting the implement now with concentration and precision. It felt like he was digging a hole straight into my brain. I started to scream and scream and scream. It felt like he was killing me.

When the hot oozing gush of blood started pouring down my earlobe, Gary seemed satisfied and his weight lifted off me. My hand flew up automatically to my ear and I felt the thick blood pooling in my ear and slipping down my neck. Gary quickly pinned my arm back down again and turned me over to do the other side.

'Stop, stop, please stop,' I begged but he showed no mercy, just a cool determination to see the job through to the end.

By the time he was done Sandra and I were both curled up on the floor crying like babies, each of us covered in blood.

His voice now seemed to come from far away, muffled as if he was in another room, though I knew he was standing right by my head.

'You better keep those clean,' he warned. 'Because if they get infected, I can't help you. Ain't nobody going to hospital. That's a fact. You gonna have to heal yourselves Indian-style. Natural, that's the only way things are gonna happen round here.'

Then he left.

Sandra and I crawled towards each other, both weeping uncontrollably, and fell into each other's arms. There we stayed, crying and holding one another. There was nothing to say.

Once again our lives seemed to slip into a nightmarish routine that consisted of being in the basement or in the hole, being fed bread and water, watching the occasional sitcom on our television and being forced to submit to regular sex.

Except now Sandra and I had painful ears. It turned out he didn't break our eardrums but the dull ache inside my head remained for a long time afterwards.

We tried to stick to Gary's rules, make him feel good, look up to him in the way he expected. When he wasn't pleased with either of us we got punished – a beating or some time in the hole. But gradually the time between the punishments got longer and longer.

The days slid past, though we never had any real sense of time since the glare of the blub was our only light. It never went off so days and nights became the same. Our body clocks adjusted and we took small catnaps, a few hours at a time. Every new day marked a step away from my old life, a loosening of the grip of normality as Gary's bizarre underground world seemed to swallow me whole.

My way of keeping myself sane was to think of my kids, of the apartment that I had found for us, of being all together, one happy family. I'd get clean for good, I'd get a new job. We'd be together and that was all that mattered.

About a month after I arrived, I got my first bath.

Since being locked up in that basement I'd not been able to wash myself, brush my teeth or hair or clean myself in any way. We had no way to do it.

I didn't know why but suddenly one day Gary announced he was going to let us bathe.

It was my turn first – I guess because I'd been there longest – and he unlocked the padlock and led me upstairs with the chains still on.

I moved slowly, dragging the heavy chains behind me. The sound as they scraped along the floorboards was painful, like nails being dragged down a chalkboard. The house was light and strange to me now. I was so used to seeing the basement lit with just the bulb my eyes couldn't adjust properly to the sunlight coming through the windows and I had to squint to stop the light hurting them.

He led me to the second floor of the house, where he had a small bathroom, and there I could see he'd already run a bath for me.

He reattached the chain to another pipe up there and then he told me to get in the water. I was on edge – I was always on edge around Gary. You never knew what new sick method of torture he'd dreamt up, whether you could trust him or whether this was a trick.

Gently, I dipped a toe into the water. The bath was beautifully warm.

I let my foot fall to the bottom, then, steadying myself with my arm, I brought in the other foot and crouched down in the water before stretching my legs out before me.

Oh my God, the feeling was indescribable. Just heavenly. I never knew water could feel so good. I let out an involuntary moan as Gary rearranged the chains so they bunched up next to the bath, then he put down the toilet seat and sat down next to me. I tried not to look at him. I tried to focus on the wonderful sensations of the water holding me, enveloping me, soothing every bit of my skin and washing away the dirt and filth of the last month.

I sank lower down into the water and my muscles seemed to relax in the warmth – it was the first time I had experienced real warmth in months.

I let my chin fall to my chest and my face break the surface, then I ducked my head down completely and let the waters wash over me like a baptism, renewing me, making me whole again. It was so overwhelming, so cleansing, I feared I might cry. But I knew this wouldn't help me so I simply closed my eyes and let the dampness ease itself out of my eyes and mingle with the water around my face.

'Here!' Gary handed me a bar of soap. 'You can use this.'

His voice was enough to bring me to my senses. I accepted

the lime-green bar and sank it into the water, working up a lather as I spun it round in my hands. Then I started to wash myself all over, getting every bit of earth and dirt I could off my body. The smell was harsh, carbolic but it may as well have been the sweetest jasmine in the world – anything was better than that moldy, damp stench of soil that had filled my nostrils every waking hour this past month.

I didn't know how long I was in there for. It felt as if I'd almost gone into some trance as I methodically worked my hands up and down my legs, around the heels of my feet, between every single toe, under my armpits and around the outside of my arms, over my belly, down my hips, up to my face and around my cheeks to my ears then back round my head and down my neck.

I used the soap to get my hair washed too, though I'd no comb or brush so my poor hair was stuck up in all strange ways, badly tangled and broken off from the number of times he'd picked me up by my ponytail.

After I was done, I stood up and Gary handed me a small grey towel, no bigger really than a hand towel. But it was enough and though hard and grainy against my skin, I felt invigorated for having washed myself completely.

There was nothing else to put on except the same shirt I'd been wearing the whole time, so I put this over my head and Gary now undid the chains from the pipe and led me out of the bathroom. But instead of going straight downstairs again, he took me into his bedroom and had sex with me there on his strange tilted bed. His heavy, large limbs on top of me, the smell of his stale breath on my face, the mechanical pumping and coarse grunts, it nearly destroyed the wonderful tingly sensation I still had from my bath. Nearly.

Afterwards he led me back down the stairs again to the basement. He had got me going ahead of him the whole time so he could see me perfectly but I couldn't see him at all. It crossed my mind maybe I could get him now but I realized that if I made any sudden movement at all, he was going to come down on me so hard, he might just kill me. Plus, I couldn't see anything I could grab that I might be able to use as a weapon. The problem was that Gary wasn't a small guy – he was well over six feet and strong with it. So if I was going to take him on I knew I'd better make damn sure I killed him and quickly or he was going to kill me.

The cellar felt cold when we returned but I didn't let that bother me. I'd got used to being cold here – it wasn't like I could do anything about it and besides, it was hardly my primary concern.

The next day Gary took Sandra up for her bath and returned about an hour later, just like he did with me. But for that time, I was on my own in the cellar again and it felt terrible. The blank walls crowded in on me. My mind started to race and I felt my pulse quicken and panic overtake my thoughts. What if he got rid of Sandra while they were up there? What if she struggled and he killed her? Would he have to kill me next? I paced the floor distractedly, trying to work out in my mind what I would do in each scenario. Nothing was implausible anymore. Nothing was too extreme for this man.

I realized then that Sandra's presence the past few weeks had probably kept me from going completely insane. It had only been a matter of minutes and yet here I was, nearly hysterical from fear. If it wasn't for Sandra, I wouldn't have made it this far. When she returned I couldn't help but smile at her and she, like the kind soul she was, smiled right back.

After Gary left that day, I confided: 'I'm so pleased you're here. You know, when you were upstairs I was sick with worry.'

'Ha ha ha, Nicole!' she laughed.

'What?' I didn't understand. I thought I was being nice, telling her that I appreciated her being here with me.

'Yeah, well, you may be pleased but I ain't all that over-the-moon about being down here.'

'Oh yeah,' I smiled back. 'I don't mean that. I'm not pleased Gary's got you down here too. Of course! I just mean I'd go insane if you weren't here.'

'Thanks, Nicole,' she said. 'Yeah, you're all right too.'

Suddenly, I was struck by sadness. Sadness and pity – for her, for me, for this whole damn situation. The bath had made me feel almost normal again, reminded me of the life I'd left behind.

'I'll get us out of here, Sandra. I promise you. I'll find a way.'

'I believe you, Nicole. I think you'll do it.'

* * *

It was a few days before Christmas when Gary asked me when my period was due.

'What day is it?' I asked.

'The 20th,' he replied.

The 20th of December? I couldn't believe it. I did some quick calculations and with a sinking heart I realized that I had missed it. This was horrific to me. If I got out, how could I raise a child from this monster alongside my precious babies? But then, possibly being pregnant could mean that Gary might treat me better.

'It should have come on the 17th,' I said, trying to keep my voice as neutral as possible.

'Really?' Gary grinned for the first time since I'd known him. It was a sinister, self-satisfied grin. He started to hum to himself then as, for the next few hours, he worked away at the hole, building up a sweat, digging away as the mounds of earth piled up around him. Just as he was leaving he said: 'I guess my plan is working out just fine then.'

Chapter Seven

Lisa

'Coming down!' Gary called from the top of the steps that led into the basement.

It was two days later and Sandra and I were in the basement, lying down on the air mattress. We looked up to see Gary bringing down a girl – a naked black girl with her hands cuffed behind her, just like Sandra and me.

The girl was crying but Gary seemed oblivious, as if there was nothing unusual in the whole situation.

'This here is Lisa,' he said curtly, indicating the crying girl, then he set to work with the muffler clamps on her ankles and the Krazy Glue, just as he did before.

All the while he was chattering away. 'I got to start wearing my glasses. I nearly picked up a man! There's this girl who jumps in my car – and she's wearing a dress so I just assume of course that she's female. Well, we start talking and then the girl pulls up her dress – and the dude has a dick!'

Gary started laughing and shaking his head at the thought.

'Oh man! I swear I had no idea. I take one look at that thing and I say: "Oh no – you got to go! I'm not into that. Get out of my car!"'

'That was not a pleasant experience. Luckily, it wasn't long before I see Lisa here and she's just crazy about my car. Isn't that right, Lisa?'

By now Gary had the clamps screwed on tight, the chain attached and padlocked to the water pipe and he was opening up the hole to put Lisa inside.

Meanwhile, she was weeping and sobbing, as you would expect. She looked young too, much younger than me and Sandra.

Once Gary went back upstairs, Sandra and I called out to her.

'I'm Nicole and this is Sandra,' I said, dipping my head close to the board so she could hear me. 'You're gonna be okay. Don't worry. He just puts you in the hole to begin with and soon you'll be out. As long as you do what he says there ain't gonna be any problems. Don't cry. I promise. It won't be too bad.'

She was still sniffling a little but after a few hours she quietened down and it wasn't long before Gary was back down in the basement, letting her up to be with us.

He gave us all some bread and water and then he lay us all down to have sex with us. This time, he laid me down first, then Sandra and finally Lisa.

Now that he thought I was pregnant I realized that he didn't want to come inside me – he was concentrating on Lisa. So he had sex with me a little first, then Sandra and he finished up with Lisa. She submitted, just like we did.

Before he went back up, he gave Lisa a shirt to put on. She accepted it without question and then watched him warily as he ascended the stairs.

'What's going on?' she demanded as soon as he was out of sight.

I placed my finger on my lips – we knew better than to start blabbing before we could be sure he wasn't standing on the other side of the door upstairs.

Now that our ears had been deadened we found our voices were quite loud and we realized he could hear us talking if he was near the basement door.

The floorboards creaked as he moved away and then I spoke. 'He's nuts. He's got this plan that he's going to keep ten women down here and get us all pregnant and then we're all going to have his babies down here in this basement.

'He thinks I might already be pregnant – I've been here the longest, about a month already. Sandra's been here about three weeks. She knew him before – they used to be friends. It's not too bad, like we say, as long as you're quiet and compliant. He don't like screaming and shouting.

'The thing is, you got to do what he says otherwise you get punished. He just wants you to go with the program and not complain or argue or nothing. It makes it easier for all of us that way. How did he get you? Were you tricking?'

'I'm not a hooker!' Lisa shot back.

'No? Well, I am. That's how he got me.'

'I just liked his car and he seemed really nice.'

Lisa was on her way to a friend's house when she noticed his Cadillac pulling slowly down Lehigh Avenue on the north side of Philly. He waved at her and she waved back. It was enough encouragement to Gary – he pulled up alongside her and asked if she was dating.

When she told him she wasn't a hooker, he offered her a lift instead.

'I liked his car,' she wailed, now obviously regretting being seduced by a flashy set of wheels.

'How old are you?' I asked.

'Nineteen,' she sniffed.

'You got kids?'

'Two – they're at home with my mom. How can I stay down here? What about my kids? It's gonna be Christmas in three days! It's so cold down here. Why haven't we got nothing more to wear than a shirt each? What about pants?'

Lisa's mind was jumping from one thing to another but I managed to get her to focus enough to carry on with her story.

'So I don't think there's any harm in letting him give me a lift to my friend's house and I'm thinking she'll be real impressed when I roll up in this sweet thing! He didn't look mean – he looked really nice.

'Anyway, we get there and I have to get a pair of gloves I've left there and he says he'll wait for me, which suits me fine because as he's down there waiting, I can show my friend this beautiful car waiting outside for me.

'I get back down to him and he asks if I want to get something to eat so I say "Yeah, why not?" and he takes me to TGI Friday's, which is a nice joint.

'I get a cheeseburger and fries and while we're eating he asks me if I want to go to Atlantic City with him tomorrow. I'm thinking like maybe this guy is a secret millionaire or something because he don't dress too well but he's got a nice car and seems to have plenty of cash to throw around on meals and trips.

'I'm thinking about it and I think, yeah, well, I'd like to go to Atlantic City but I tell him I don't have anything to wear. I mean, I'm wearing just my ordinary jeans and I don't have any change of clothes.

'So then he pulls out a fifty-dollar bill and he tells me we're gonna go shopping afterwards to Sears and he's gonna buy me some clothes. Well, that's a pretty nice offer, so I accept and he gets me a couple pairs of jeans and two tops. Then he says: "Can I put them on you?"

'And I guess because now he's spent a bit of dough on me and I trust him I say "yes" so he brings me back to this place, which I got to say is a bit of a disappointment because by now I'm expecting him to live in a really nice big house in the good part of town.

'Anyway, he gives me a wine cooler and I start to play the pinball machine in his dining room. Then he puts a film on the VCR – *Splash* – and I start to watch it while he's disappeared upstairs. But you see I took an allergy pill at the restaurant and with the wine, it's making me real drowsy.

'The next thing I know I'm laying on his bed upstairs completely naked and he's having sex with me.

'I don't feel that good about all this now so then I ask him to take me back to my girlfriend's house. And I'm just getting up to put on my clothes and that's when he starts choking me.'

Lisa's hands flew up to her throat at the memory.

'He's got his arm round my throat and I can't breathe and I manage to say: "Okay! Okay – quit choking me, I'll do whatever you want."

'Then he cuffs me and brings me down here.'

Sandra and me were nodding – it was just like he did with us two.

We liked Lisa immediately. She was young and friendly and she seemed to adjust pretty well to her new situation. Lisa's two kids were with her mom and they got supported through welfare – she dropped out of school in eleventh grade when she fell pregnant and she never completed her high school diploma.

She was uneducated but she was no fool and she quickly caught on to the right way to speak to Gary without getting him angry. I guess the fact that Sandra and I were there to reassure her helped a lot. For our part, it was nice to have extra company and since it was now nearing Christmas we talked a lot about our families and our kids. It helped to be able to tell others about the ones we were missing. I loved telling them about Toya's funny ways and Zornae's sweet innocence. And I could speak for hours and hours about

Ricky, even though he was just a tiny baby when I last saw him. I loved talking about them, but it was painful too – they change by the minute in those early days, growing up before your eyes! And I was missing out. That was hard to accept.

I appreciated talking to Lisa and Sandra so much. I knew for certain that if I was on my own down here I'd have probably lost my mind. Added to that was the fear that I was now carrying Gary's child.

A baby with this cruel man! The thought was horrific.

By now Gary was coming down and spending a lot of time with us girls – I could see he was enjoying having company. It wasn't like we were going anywhere and we all just nodded and agreed with him most of the time so he was getting all the things he wanted.

Now that there were three of us, he'd started to rank us in order of how long we've been there. Since I'd been there the longest I got to spend most of my time up top. But he still put Sandra and Lisa in the hole whenever he went out. The hole wasn't big enough for three. And perhaps he felt he'd 'broken me in'. Who knows? I reckon he'd got fed up digging because he didn't bother any more.

I tried speaking to him nice to get him to like me. A couple of times I complimented him on his shirt and he seemed pleased with that.

I didn't know what my plan was yet but I knew for certain that there was only one way out of here and that was through him, so I had to get him to trust me.

Sandra trusted me. She was confident I would find a way out for all of us and I wasn't going to let her down.

Chapter Eight

Christmas

I woke up on Christmas morning with a heavy heart.

In all my life, I don't think I'd ever felt so low. My Christmases of the past had been special, wonderful times and even more magical since Toya reached the age of being able to appreciate the day, the presents and all the things that made it fun.

My mind slipped back to the Christmas before, when I still had my kids with me and life was good.

That Christmas when I awoke my eyes scanned the room – Toya's bed was empty. I looked over to the crib to see that she had climbed in and she was trying to feed the baby strawberry yoghurt. That kid had an obsession with strawberry yoghurt!

The crib was smeared and spattered with creamy pink gloop – it looked like she'd tried to repaint the whole crib with the stuff!

'How many times I got to tell you about that yoghurt?' I demanded.

'Morning Mommy! Happy Christmas!' she smiled, aiming a dripping spoon at the tiny baby's mouth. At this point Zornae was just weeks old.

But her big sister Toya loved her so much she couldn't keep away from her.

'Yeah, yeah. Happy Christmas honey,' I sighed, lifting her out of the crib and going to get a cloth to wipe the baby. Robert was sleeping off a hangover, the presents were stacked under a small plastic tree, a few baubles and tinsel brightened up an otherwise small apartment.

In this moment we had everything to look forward to – gifts, dinner with my mom, a whole day of fun and games.

* * *

Looking back I couldn't believe how drastically my life had gone wrong in the space of one year. Not long after Christmas Robert and me split up, then I found out I was expecting Ricky.

I was now going out to work every day to try and make a living and leaving my sister Iris in charge of the kids. That's when I lost Zornae to child protective services who claimed she wasn't getting appropriate care.

Zornae had got a weight problem so I was feeding her up with all these different formulas but she was still skinny as a rake and child protective services saw that she was too thin and accused me of neglecting to feed her properly.

I had to go through the courts and that's when my doctor confirmed that Zornae was born thin and her skinniness was down to her medical problems.

He confirmed I'd been back and forth with her, trying out all these different formulas and vitamins and stuff. Child protective services were forced to admit they'd got it wrong but they still weren't happy with where I was living so they said I had to find a more suitable place to stay before they'd give her back.

I was mad as hell at Iris but what could I do?

So then I just had Toya with me and I couldn't depend on Iris to look after her. I had to give up my job and the only work I could do was hooking.

To my eternal shame, I took up crack after a break of a year to cope. I was still trying to take care of Toya and her dad was making it really difficult to arrange our visitations properly. I'd let him have her for a day or so and then, instead of bringing her back to me on time, he stopped bringing her back at all or he brought her back so late I'd have to wait for hours and hours. It was driving me mad.

One day in July she was meant to be back at home with me but of course her dad had failed to return her.

So I asked Iris to come with me to their place on Augustus Avenue so we could confront Billy about what was going on.

We got to the house that he shared with his mom Clara and as we were coming down the street, I saw Toya playing on her big wheel outside by herself. I took her aside and at that moment I saw the trolley car coming down the street.

'You take Toya back to my house,' I instructed Iris. 'I've got to go and tell Billy we've got her. I need to sort this out once and for all. He's messing me around like crazy.'

'No,' Iris objected. 'We got her now. You don't need to go down there.'

'I got to talk to him!' I insisted. 'For one thing, he's going to be worried if Toya doesn't come back. At the least I got to tell him she's with me. Just get her on the trolley and I'll be home soon.'

So I walked down the street, leaving Toya and Iris standing there, thinking she was going to take her on the trolley.

I got to Billy and Clara's home and I let them know that I had Toya and she was coming back with me. But they weren't happy and we started fighting about how they were making it difficult and never dropping her off on time.

As I was arguing with Clara, Billy slipped out of the house, got in his station wagon and saw that Iris and Toya were still waiting for me on the corner. They didn't get on the trolley.

Billy drove up to the pair and made a grab for Toya. She screamed and Iris was hollering too but he just put our daughter in the car and drove off.

By the time I got outside it was all over.

'Why didn't you do something?' I yelled at Iris, still standing in the street. 'You should have run after him.'

'I didn't have the right shoes on.'

They had taken my baby and now I was all alone. I couldn't believe how quickly it had happened.

I didn't have the money to go through the courts and even if I did, I knew that child protective services wouldn't be on my side right then. So that's why getting the apartment was so crucial. If I had a place to stay, I could get Zornae and Ricky back with me and then I had a decent chance of getting Toya too.

Now I was in this hellhole and my hopes of getting my children back were all but gone. Every step I'd taken since leaving my apartment that night of Thanksgiving had taken me further and further away from my kids.

All I wanted in the world was to see their faces again.

I put my head down and sent up a silent prayer to all my children, hoping they were safe and well somewhere and they were being taken care of.

Mommy loves you, I told them. *Mommy loves you all and I'll be home soon.*

I promise.

I thought of my mom again – she'd be beside herself by now. We usually spoke on the phone every day – it had been over a month and though I occasionally dropped off the radar for a few days we'd never gone this long without speaking.

I'm sorry Mom, I whispered to myself. *I'm so sorry Mom.*

In my head I heard her replying: *You got yourself into this mess, Josefina. You got to find a way to get out.*

My head was clear for the first time in ages and I came to the horrible realization that she was right; I was partly to blame for being in this place. Sure, this guy was a nut, but I couldn't run away from the fact that I also had my part to play in all this.

If I hadn't stepped out that night, I wouldn't be in this situation. I'd made so many bad choices the past few years, taken so many wrong turns, I wondered if there was ever going to be a way back for me. I prayed to God for the chance to try. I just wanted a chance to put this right, a chance to get my family back.

Maybe I couldn't get everything straight again but I had to try. If Mom was here, that's exactly what she would say. And she'd be right.

I had to do everything in my power to get out.

* * *

None of us were talking much – I could see the same depressing realization had struck us all. It was Christmas yet none of us were with our loved ones.

Lisa was missing her kids, Sandra her mom and sister.

What kind of a Christmas was this? Stuck in this basement with no daylight, half starved and naked, sore from being chained up and filthy as dogs.

On the radio the announcer wished us all a merry Christmas and then, almost to underline our collective misery he played: 'All I Want for Christmas is You'.

I had to resist the urge to melt into tears. I didn't want to bring my bad feeling to these other girls, didn't want to make them feel any worse than I knew they already felt. But it sure was hard to keep my head up.

Suddenly I heard the click of the door to the basement and Gary's footsteps coming down the stairs.

'Happy Christmas Girls!' he said cheerfully.

'Happy Christmas, Gary,' we chimed back, but there wasn't much heart in it.

'Look, seeing as it's Christmas I decided to treat you all to a Chinese meal. Here are menus – you can have one dish each.'

He looked pleased with himself, proud at his generosity.

We each took a menu from his local Chinese restaurant and started reading down the list. It had been so long since I'd tasted any real food except plain white bread that my mouth was salivating just looking over the menu: sweet and sour pork balls, griddled dumplings, wonton soup, chicken chow mein.

Oh my God, it all looked so delicious.

Now Lisa, Sandra and myself were all looking at each other excitedly.

'What are you going to get?' Lisa asked me.

'I don't know. I haven't got to the end of the menu yet. It all looks so good.'

'I know, I know!'

My eyes could hardly take it all in. How can you decide what to eat when you're starving and someone hands you a menu? You want it all!

'I like chow mein,' Sandra said simply. 'Can you get me that Gary, please?'

Lisa chose stir-fried beef and eventually, after a lot of thinking, I settled on shrimp fried rice.

Gary went upstairs and within half an hour he was back down again, this time carrying a bag of take-out that I could smell before he'd even set foot in the basement.

The aroma was incredible and my stomach ached with

hunger. Now we were all sitting up, eager to devour our Christmas feast.

Gary handed out plastic forks and our boxes with foil lids. We ripped them off and I was almost overcome with the smell – it was the first real food I'd had in a month and I was dizzy just thinking about it.

'Oh sweet Jesus!' exclaimed Sandra.

'Yeah!' breathed Lisa, taking in the heady scent. She'd only been here three days but it was enough time on bread and water to feel sick with hunger.

I looked up at them both, my rice still untouched, unwilling to break into the food until we were all ready. The other girls were smiling, and I smiled back.

In that instant, and for the first time in a month, I felt normal. Just normal.

I couldn't wait any longer. I dug my fork into the soft, golden rice and took a bite. Oh my Lord, the sensations exploded in my mouth. It was like nothing I'd ever experienced before – sweet, salty, spicy, fragrant, sour, fresh and tangy. I felt like I was eating for the first time in my life. I took another mouthful. It was so good it wasn't long before I was digging in over and over again, ravenous.

After ten minutes of silent eating I looked up to see Gary sitting at the table, watching us all – his expression was blank, unreadable.

'Gary, this sure is good,' I said, appreciatively. 'You want to try some?'

'No thanks,' he said. 'It's yours. I ate already.'

Sandra looked at me. 'Can I try some please, Nicole?'

'Sure.'

Sandra took a forkful of rice and placed it carefully in her mouth, then, because she had a strange problem with her jaw, she worked the rice around and around in her mouth, slowly and carefully. It took Sandra ten minutes to finish every mouthful but she seemed so happy right now.

She offered me some chow mein and I eagerly accepted.

We each tried a forkful of each other's food before setting to work on our own dishes again. My belly was full long before I stopped eating but there was nothing on earth that was going to stop me finishing every grain of rice in that foil carton.

When we were done, we sat there, all of us groaning and holding our stomachs, happy and full.

The food was wonderful but best of all, just the ordinary feeling of eating a meal, a normal meal, lifted our spirits.

Gary let us sit there for a while before ordering us all to lie down to have sex with him – it was the last thing I wanted but I didn't object.

This time, when he got on top of me, his heavy frame pushed down hard on my stomach, making me feel like I might throw up.

'You look fatter,' he said to me as he was leaving, clearly happy with himself. 'It's good. It suits you.'

I looked down at my skinny legs and thin arms – I couldn't see any difference from how I was when he brought me down here a month ago. All my life I'd been naturally slim and the drugs had definitely kept me on the skinnier side. Now perhaps he saw the bulge in my belly from the food and assumed this meant I was gaining weight.

Maybe I was gaining weight from being off the drugs, I didn't know. Maybe it was because I *was* pregnant – my period still hadn't arrived. There were no other signs, however.

It was Gary's attitude that riled me. It was incredible that this man actually thought he was doing me a favor! I wondered if this was how he treated Anjeanette when she was pregnant. No wonder they took the baby off him.

Lisa was talking now, telling a story about an old boyfriend. The food had made her chatty.

'He wanted to marry me,' she said. 'I said no – I didn't really love him. He was sweet though. I wish now I'd said yes to him and no to Gary. Boy, I sure did get that the wrong way round. I got no clue how to pick men!'

She laughed at herself and I couldn't help but smile.

'What about you, Nicole?' she asked. 'You ever been married?'

'Sure,' I said. 'Ronnie. Nice guy, lovely guy actually. He was good to me – set me up in a nice home, paid for everything. But you know, I don't think marriage suited me much.

'He went out to work every day, making tile. I stayed home and looked after Toya, cleaned the house, you know, the usual, boring stuff.

'Twice a week, we went out – once to the pictures, once to a restaurant. It was the same week in, week out. Not my cup of tea. I lasted a few months and then we packed it in – I told him I wasn't happy and he accepted that. He was so good to me, didn't make a fuss, didn't make it difficult for me to leave. We just went our separate ways. It was hard on Toya though – she was three at the time and she loved her daddy Ron.'

'You wish you had stayed?' asked Sandra.

I thought for a minute.

'No. No, it was the right thing to do. I mean, if I had stayed any longer I would have got more and more miserable and then I would have made Ron miserable too. And that would have been much worse than the way we left things, as friends. As it was, there wasn't any big fight or rows. He sent me off with a smile and I'm pleased we both kept things pleasant. I don't know. Maybe I'm just not the marrying kind.'

Sandra sighed. 'Nobody's ever asked me to marry them,' she said sadly. I knew what she wasn't saying – that maybe nobody would.

'Don't worry Sandra,' Lisa said comfortingly. 'They will one day.'

Sandra looked up gratefully at Lisa. 'You think so?'

'I know so!' Lisa laughed. 'Some day your handsome prince is going to get down on one knee and give you a rock so big your hand is going to fall off just trying to keep the damn thing on!'

We all started giggling and Sandra gave Lisa a playful push.

It turned out to be a good day after all.

Chapter Nine

Deborah

It was late at night when Deborah Dudley arrived, and the manner of her entrance set the tone of her whole incarceration.

Unlike with the other girls, Deborah wasn't crying when she was brought down in handcuffs and naked.

No, Deborah was mad, real mad, and she was screaming and shouting and cussing Gary out like she couldn't believe he had the cheek to lock her up.

Deborah was black, like the others, but she was much darker than the rest and not real pretty like Lisa or sweet like Sandra. No, Deborah seemed hard.

'What the fuck do you think you're doing, you little shit?' she screamed at Gary as he started to work on the muffler clamps.

He didn't reply, just kept on going.

'Are you deaf? You fucking freak?' she screamed at him again. Then, when she didn't get a response she looked round at all of us sitting downstairs in chains, watching her in silence.

'Whatcha ya'll lookin' at, bitches?' she shouted. 'You got something to say about all of this? Let me out of here, you bastard!' she addressed herself to Gary once more but by now he had the chain attached and he was lifting the bags off the board over the hole.

When he'd opened it up he pointed inside and ordered Deborah: 'Get in!'

'Uh-uh.' She shook her head defiantly.

'Get in the hole!' he said.

'No, I'm not getting in there. I don't want to be down there.'

I wanted to tell her to just shut up and do as she was told, that she was just making things harder for herself. She didn't seem to grasp what was going on here.

She just kept on refusing until Gary grabbed hold of a shovel handle and started beating her behind hard with it. She was cowering now, trying to protect herself from the blows, but I could see she was still objecting.

Finally, exasperated, Gary just pushed her inside the hole and quickly slid the board over the top, weighing it down again with the bags.

'Stupid bitch,' he exclaimed, more in frustration than anger, then he headed back upstairs again.

Once we were sure Gary was out of earshot we called out to Deborah, trying to reassure her and tell her what was going on.

It was the night before New Year and now there were four of us locked up in that cellar in North Marshall Street.

I used to believe that the way you start a year is the same way you're going to finish it but I couldn't let myself think like that in here. If I believed I was going to spend a whole year in this prison then I'd go mad.

Meanwhile, Deborah was keeping us all up with a lot of shouting and hollering – she was asking us to let her out of the hole.

'We can't let you out,' we told her. 'If he finds out we'll all get punished. Just make things easy on yourself and quieten down otherwise you're going to make him mad.'

But Deborah didn't quieten down – she never quietened down. And she ended up bringing a whole ton of trouble down on her own head and ours too.

Deborah Dudley had had a hard life. We found out later she'd been brought up in the Richard Allen Projects, a large, run-down government housing estate riddled with crime and drugs.

Deborah had been abused all her life – she had grown up quickly and learned to fight to survive.

She wasn't pretty and she wasn't that smart either. Deborah hadn't had a whole lot of options in her life so she was working the streets when Gary picked her up, though neither of them said where that was.

The thing was – Deborah didn't know any other way than to fight so when she found herself in Gary's sex dungeon she thought she could fight her way out.

Every moment of every day from the time she arrived, she fought Gary. She refused to get in the hole, she didn't want to submit to sex and she shouted and yelled at him all the time. She shouted and yelled even when he wasn't there.

Ordinarily, I would have admired Deborah's refusal to be beaten down by Gary. She refused to give in. But it was tiring for the rest of us being around that level of aggression and anger all the time because it made us all nervous in case we all got punished.

'All he wants is for us to submit to his plan,' I told her, outlining his crazy idea of us all having his babies down in the cellar. 'If you just do as he says you'll be okay.'

But Deborah never submitted. It was bad enough being locked up in the cellar and now Deborah was making it harder.

She provoked Gary into beating her so much and now, instead of doing it himself, he ordered us to do it. I guess it was part of his sick idea of creating rank in our group; maybe he got the idea from his time in the army, I didn't know. All I knew was that it was horrific to me. I'd never beaten anyone in my life before.

But Gary wanted to ensure complete obedience, to establish his total authority over us, and so when he ordered me to beat Deborah, it was one of the hardest things I'd ever had to do.

'You beat her now with this,' he said, handing me the wooden stick. 'And you make sure to do it hard. That girl's got an ass like leather. She won't feel a thing unless you give her a decent whack.'

So now I took up the stick and steeled myself to approach Deborah.

'Don't you hit me with that damn thing!' she warned.

'I'm gonna bust your ass real bad if you touch me just once with that.'

I tried to ignore her as I took the stick, pulled my arm back and landed a blow on her thigh. She started hollering but I didn't rest until I'd hit her five or six times. I wanted to do it hard and quick – get it over with.

I didn't even think to object. If I had, Gary would have beaten me instead, or worse. And I was still hoping I could gain his trust. Mind you, since Deborah arrived, I couldn't tell if it was working. He seemed so wound up and frustrated a lot of the time now and he kept trying to think of different ways to punish her.

'I just don't know what to beat her with anymore!' he exploded one day. 'She's got a hide so hard nothing makes any difference.'

After Gary returned upstairs I went over to her to try and give her a hug.

'I'm sorry, Deborah. We've just got to do as he says,' I explained. 'Can't you see that you're making things worse for yourself by objecting all the time?'

Deborah accepted the hug but she was still mad, spitting mad.

'Why didn't you take the stick and just hit him with it?' she said. 'You could have beat him round the head and then we could all get out of here.'

She was gesturing wildly now, her hands flew to her head like she couldn't believe I could be so stupid. In her mind it was all so simple.

'We wouldn't be able to get out,' I explained patiently. It was like talking to a child. 'He keeps all the keys to the padlocks upstairs so once he was unconscious, we wouldn't have any way of getting the chains off. It would be more dangerous that way – we could starve.'

'It's true,' Lisa chimed in. 'Gary doesn't get visitors. It would only take a few days and then we'd all die of hunger and thirst.'

'This is bullshit!' shouted Deborah. 'All you bitches are pussies! How come none of you found a way out of here yet? If we all keep yelling someone's gonna hear us and then they'll come and get us.'

I'd been in the basement for around seven weeks by this point and I knew there was no chance. I told Deborah about how the radios stopped the neighbors from hearing us, how I nearly escaped and lay out in the yard for twenty minutes yelling and still no one came. I told her how Gary had paid off all the drug dealers in the area so no one bothered him. Still, Deborah refused to submit.

So Deborah spent most of her time in the hole – she was just on bread and water while the rest of us were now getting a bit of variety in our diet. Occasionally Gary brought down canned soup with crackers, noodles, waffles, hot dogs or cheese sandwiches. It made a nice change from bread and water but it just made Deborah even madder to see us with it. Nothing seemed to calm her down and she thought she had a whole load of plans to get us out of there.

'Let's jump him,' she suggested for about the sixth time

that day. 'If one of us stands by the bottom of the steps and another one on the other side we can easily overpower him and knock him out with the stick.'

'Yeah?' I said. 'And then what? How are we going to get out of here? Like I said a million times, he doesn't bring the keys for the padlocks down with him so how are we supposed to get out of the basement? How many times have I got to tell you – no one knows we're here!'

'We'll figure something out.'

'That's not good enough – I'm not going to risk starving to death on a plan we haven't thought through. I'm not risking my life on some stupid, half-baked idea which won't work.'

'She's right,' Sandra said to Deborah. 'How are we going to get out? If we want an escape plan we've got to know how we're going to escape. Not just how we're going to take him out. And just suppose we don't manage to knock him out, he might decide to kill us all for attacking him.'

'Shuddup, Sandra!' Deborah retorted. 'You just stay out of this. This is between me and Nicole.'

'I'm just saying – you should listen to Nicole,' said Sandra, quietly now, cowed by Deborah's vast temper. 'She's got her head screwed on. She says she's gonna find a way out for us. You're just making everything worse for yourself.'

'At least I'm not weak and giving in to everything like you lot!' Deborah spat. 'We gotta try to have a plan. If you all listen to Nicole here you'll be down here for the rest of your lives.'

Not for the first time I got a sense that Deborah didn't appreciate the seriousness of our situation.

She seemed to think she could just punch her way out. It wasn't that simple – Gary was a cold, calculating son of a bitch. He was going to keep right on going until she gave in. She couldn't win this way.

'If you keep fighting him like you're going those punishments are just going to get worse and worse,' I said. 'Who knows what he might do? He's not right in the head. You've got to realize that.'

'Oh, I suppose I'm going to die here, aren't I?' Deborah shot back sarcastically.

'Yeah – pretty much!' I screamed at her now.

That shut her up.

That night we all got some proper rest for the first time in ages. I hoped I'd got through to her. I was just trying to stay strong and focused on getting Gary to like me and I knew Deborah resented the fact that I didn't get beaten anymore or put in the hole but she hadn't seen what I'd been through already, none of them had.

Years later that conversation replayed over and over in my mind.

'I'm going to die here, aren't I?' I heard Deborah saying.

'Yeah, pretty much!' I replied, meaning, 'If you keep doing what you're doing.'

That was all.

I wanted her to understand that I meant she would die there if she carried on the way she was going. I wanted to get through to her, make her understand that she could choose how this went for her.

How was I to know at this stage what was going to happen to Deborah? How could any of us know just how sick Gary Heidnik was?

I knew in my heart that he was capable of anything – but in the end the horrors he visited on us were worse than anything I could ever have imagined.

* * *

The next day Deborah was sulking. Now Gary came down to have sex with us   since Sandra hadn't had her period either he assumed she must be pregnant too and now, when he lay us down to have sex with us, it was Lisa or Deborah at the end. Afterwards, he handed out cookies to us all, cheap supermarket cookies with vanilla on one side, chocolate on another and cream in the middle – we got two apiece. The sweet cream and crunch of the biscuits were wonderful but it wasn't enough to fill us up.

Gary didn't talk much anymore – he seemed locked into Deborah's non-stop dramas, intent on getting her to give in to him.

He went to put her in the hole again before he left but she refused.

'I'm just going to wear your butt out beating it,' he sighed, picking up the stick again.

We went through the same routine of him beating her and then she finally got in the hole.

After he left I erupted at her. 'I don't understand this, Deborah. Please explain – what part of this aren't you getting?'

'If you think I'm just going to sit here quietly and take this shit, forget it!' Deborah yelled. 'For. Get. It!'

She started mumbling to herself and I could only catch snippets of her train of thought: 'Damn stupid bitch... Lording it over the rest of us... Thinks she's better than us... bullshit...'

She yelled at me again. 'You ain't no better than me, Nicole! You just taking it like a bitch. You hear me? You're just taking it!'

'Yeah, yeah. I hear you Deborah,' I sighed.

It seemed I'd failed to get through to her again. I stopped talking – I just didn't know what to say to her anymore.

Chapter Ten
Jacqueline

It was January 18, the day before my birthday, and we knew that there was someone else in the house.

We'd heard Gary's familiar heavy footfall on the porch and this time it was accompanied by another set of feet, lighter, quicker than his.

Sure enough, twenty minutes later, he came down with a small skinny girl in shackles who was almost skipping down the steps next to him.

'This here is Jacqueline!' said Gary. 'Jacqueline – meet the girls. That's Nicole, Deborah, Sandra and Lisa.'

We all nodded towards her as she looked at each of us in turn, confused and upset, but not bawling.

Gary was now doing her muffler clamps but Jacqueline was so small her feet just slipped right through them. So he put handcuffs on her ankles instead – now he was chatting away as if recounting a day at the office.

'I was out on the northside looking for a girl and I see some hooker in front of one of the hotels so I stop to pick her up. Anyway, she's about to get in the car when Jacqueline here comes racing over from the other side of the street, shouting: "Don't pick her! Don't pick her! She's got AIDS! Pick me!" It's freezing cold and she's jumping up and down shouting to pick her – so, you know, I let her in the car.'

Jacqueline was rolling her eyes now as Gary told the story, like she couldn't believe she'd done that.

Gary motioned for Jacqueline to get down into the hole and though she obviously didn't want to, she eventually got in, squatting down at first to get her balance, then swinging her little legs in and then crouching down inside it.

He pulled the board over the top as he kept on speaking: 'So then Jacqueline here gets in the car instead of the other girl and I take her back.'

Just then we heard Jacqueline shouting up through the board: 'She doesn't have AIDS! I lied – she doesn't have AIDS!'

This made Gary laugh out loud and a few of us smiled despite the appalling situation.

Jacqueline, who later told us she was eighteen, seemed to have no concept of danger, no sense of entering a hellish new reality. We didn't want her to feel bad so we all just let her talk, telling her little about the punishments we'd all been subjected to. We only told her about Gary's plan and she listened, her eyes wide with shock like we were recounting a story about someone else.

'No way!' she exclaimed. 'That is so weird. Isn't that weird? What's this guy on?'

We told her – Thorazine. But we didn't tell her the worst. It felt mean somehow. She'd find out soon enough. Even Deborah was quiet – I wondered if she felt sorry for Jacqueline. I did. Eighteen is no age.

Suddenly something occurred to Jacqueline.

'I just bought some new shoes!' she exclaimed. 'Oh damn! I bet somebody else be stealing them now!'

I wanted to laugh. That was what Jacqueline was worried about. Shoes!

The next day everything changed for me – and strangely enough, it was all down to a pair of shoes.

Well, slippers, actually.

We were all sitting round talking when we heard the door to the basement opening up – Gary came down with the Chinese menus again.

'Seeing as it's Nicole's birthday today you're all gonna get a special treat. One dish each! Happy Birthday Nicole!'

Until this moment I'd been trying to forget that it was my birthday, that I was turning twenty-six chained up in a cellar in a madman's house. I must have told Gary some time in my early days there – I didn't even remember when. It had been almost two months since Gary abducted me, and there was still no sign of my period. I was convinced I was pregnant.

'Thank you, Gary – that's so sweet of you,' I said, smiling at him warmly.

It was a start, I thought. He remembered my birthday. That meant he was thinking about me. I ordered Pork Yuk, minced pork in lettuce leaves, and the others chose their dishes.

This time, when he came back down with the food, he was juggling a number of other items.

'Today, because it's your birthday, we're gonna have a party for you!' he told me. 'I've bought a cake and a present.'

If I'd ever had a weirder birthday than this one before, I certainly couldn't remember it. There we were, five half-naked, half-starved women chained in a basement – and we were having a party. Unbelievable.

But I didn't care – in this moment I felt something shift, a change in the balance of power.

He was thinking about me. He liked me. I didn't care that the other girls were giving me daggers – it's what I would have expected. For the first time I sensed that Gary liked me and I wasn't going to blow it.

Trying to ignore the fact that I was still chained in his dungeon, I tried to act as normally as possible, like a girl being treated on her birthday.

'Oh wow, Gary. You didn't have to go to all this trouble,' I said, smiling at him. We wolfed down our Chinese meals and then afterwards Gary led the girls in a round of 'Happy Birthday' and we each got a slice of cake.

It was soft and spongy, oozing with thick buttercream and jam. The sugary icing was intoxicating.

'And, this is for you,' Gary said, smiling shyly now as he handed me a box covered in purple wrapping paper. There was even a bow.

He went to a lot of trouble.

I didn't have to fake it, I was genuinely surprised, and set to ripping at the paper.

I got the lid off the box to reveal a pair of red, furry slippers.

I put them on straight away. God, they felt so good! Until now we'd all been walking on cold, solid concrete, numbing the soles of our feet, keeping our legs almost permanently chilled.

They were just a pair of slippers but they made me feel like a queen.

'Oh wow!' I exclaimed again. 'These are so nice. They feel real good, Gary. Thank you!'

Gary looked satisfied – he eyed the slippers on my feet and then looked up at the other girls, as if instructing them silently to admire them.

Of course they were all green with envy, except maybe Sandra who just seemed happy nobody was getting beaten.

They murmured quietly, 'Nice.' 'Lovely.' 'They look real comfy.'

I looked down at them again and recalled an old film I saw once, *The Wizard of Oz*. Dorothy and her ruby slippers.

I closed my eyes, clicked the heels together three times and in my head I said: *There's no place like home, there's no place like home.*

In the film this sends Dorothy back home to her dearly loved Aunty Em. I thought of my children, thought of my mom and how wonderful it would be to see them again.

Would my wish come true? I opened my eyes. Gary was still standing there, grinning away.

* * *

Later, Gary uncorked some non-alcoholic apple cider and we drank that out of Styrofoam cups. It was unpleasantly sweet and sharp enough to make me wince.

The music still blared out the radio – Prince's 'Purple Rain' came on. A few of us started humming along, catching each other's eyes and smiling for what felt like the first time in ages. Our voices, though soft and quiet, came together in that moment, as we mouthed the words to ourselves.

For the first time in a long while the music actually felt like our friend, not our enemy.

Then they played 'Stand By Me'.

'I like this one,' Gary said, looking at me. 'Let's dance.'

So I stood up and walked into my captor's embrace, letting him hold me close and turn me as we slow danced in his basement.

Me, in my new red slippers and chains.

'No I won't be afraid.' The song's lyrics were strangely comforting. 'No, I won't shed a tear…'

I felt the strength of his lean muscular body and his firm grip on my hands and this time, I didn't smile. I looked away, coyly, as I would if I knew someone liked me and I was playing hard to get. I could tell he wanted me to look at him but I held back, just a little, just enough to keep him interested.

Was I playing a game? Of course – but I was playing for my life so I couldn't put a foot wrong. I knew if I was too keen to show I liked him, he'd see right through it.

He was mad but he wasn't dumb.

This had to come across as genuine. There was no room for screw-ups.

I briefly caught his eyes; the intensity was searing. I knew now why he chose this song – he actually wanted me to stand by him!

Okay, Gary, I thought, as I looked him directly in the eyes. *You want a friend? I'll be your friend. I'll stand by you.*

* * *

Until this moment I had no idea that my plan was working. Gary hadn't given anything away, nothing to make me think I was getting through to him.

Now I knew he wanted me on his side.

And here I was, his very own Cinderella, chained up in his basement, ennobled by a pair of red fluffy slippers, lifted out of the darkness towards the light, towards freedom, back to my mom, back to my children.

I still didn't know what my plan was – there was nothing organized about it, nothing clear-cut. I just knew I had to keep going along the same lines, get him to like me, get him to trust me.

If he thought for a minute that he'd lost me, I would pay with my life.

Chapter Eleven

Losing Sandra

'Get up, Sandra! Come on, girl, stand up! Wake up!'

It must have been early February, but I'm not sure of the exact date. Sandra was hanging from the rafter by her wrist – she'd not eaten now for a couple of days and Gary was punishing her.

He'd chained her by her arm to a rafter in the ceiling so that she was forced to stand with one arm held over her head.

But she'd been standing like this for nearly a day now and at some point she'd fallen into unconsciousness – her whole body was slumped towards the floor, suspended just by her wrist.

Earlier in the day Gary had been down, trying to force her to eat.

He put a bit of bread in her mouth.

'Come on, chew it!' he shouted at her. 'Chew the goddamn bread, Sandra!'

He got the stick and beat her across the back of her legs.

'Swallow it!' he ordered angrily. 'Swallow it!'

But Sandra just moaned and spat the bread right out again.

'Damn you, Sandra!' he shouted. 'You're gonna eat! I'll make sure of that. You're just gonna stay there until you do.'

He thought she was rebelling, faking illness so he'd left her like that, one arm held over her head. But I could see she wasn't well. She was so tired she could barely stand, let alone make the effort to chew the morsel. For Sandra, eating was always a problem but right now she seemed so out of it, she couldn't get up the energy to eat even the smallest bite of food.

Her body was slumped forwards. She wasn't moving.

I walked over to her and tried her pulse – it was beating but she was unconscious.

Her head hung low, her face sagged.

I wanted to shake her, tell her to get up, because I knew if Gary came down and found her like this again he'd only punish her more.

'Come on, Sandra, get up!' I said through gritted teeth. She was too heavy for me to lift and even if I did pick her up, it looked like she'd just fall back down again.

The other girls were calling out to her. 'Sandra! Hey, Sandra! Wake up! Get up Sandra!'

Just then we heard Gary's footsteps down the basement steps and I moved away from the suspended girl.

Gary's face was a picture of fury as he caught sight of Sandra hanging pathetically in the middle of the room.

He stood looking at her like that for a second before abruptly turning round and going back up the stairs.

Seconds later he returned with the key to her handcuffs. He shouted to her: 'Stand up, you bitch!'

Nothing.

'I'll make you stand up!' he muttered as he unlocked her handcuff and in that moment Sandra's whole body collapsed to the floor and her head hit the corner of the hole. Whack!

She lay there, still. I could see she was gone. Her mouth gaped, drool ran out the side, one eye was open, the other closed.

'Oh man, that's just a waste of a baby,' said Gary.

We all sat there in stunned silence. Sandra was dead. I could hardly believe it. In those terrible, terrifying seconds a powerful sense of grief descended on us. I fought back my tears as Gary heaved Sandra over onto her back, then he picked her up like a sack of potatoes, slung her over his shoulder, and carried her upstairs.

The door clicked and I let the tears flow freely. I couldn't believe she was gone – Sandra had been here with me almost since the very beginning.

How could she be dead?

But worse than the fact that Gary had killed her was his cold, callous reaction. He'd known Sandra for years – they were friends before this and in that one sentence he told us exactly what he thought of us all.

We were no more than baby-carriers, vessels for his children. He couldn't care less about Sandra, he just carried her upstairs like she was no more than a piece of meat.

Lisa asked a question into the silence, 'How do you think she died?'

I looked up. Her eyes were red and puffy. She was crying too. I looked around – they were all sobbing. Sandra was so soft, so innocent. Just a child, really. She should have been home with her mom and sister looking after her. She should have been kept safe somewhere. She didn't deserve this, this hideous end.

I shook my head, trying to make sense of it.

'I think she was choking on some bread,' I said slowly. 'That made her lose consciousness. Gary – he was trying to test her. I reckon he thought that if he let out the cuffs she'd put her hands out to stop herself falling. I don't think he realized or understood that she wasn't with it.'

'That bastard!' Deborah exploded. Perhaps Deborah wasn't such a hard-ass after all. I could see she was shaken up quite badly. It was as if Sandra's weaknesses and problems had brought out the soft side in all of us, even Deborah.

'Did you see her face?' said Jacqueline, her eyes wide in horror. 'She was checked out. I ain't never seen a dead person before. Poor Sandra!'

'Yeah,' Lisa echoed, lost in thought. 'Poor Sandra.'

But I could see what they were all really thinking – poor us! Which one will be next?

That night everyone was quiet, even Deborah. I was grief-stricken. What a way to die! Sandra was so young, so trusting. Tortured to death by a man she had thought was her friend. She trusted me to get her out of this prison and I'd let her down so badly. I was racked with guilt and remorse. I should have done more to help. I could have done more. I could have made her eat if I'd really tried. She didn't have to die. It all seemed so pointless and stupid. So damn stupid.

I pulled my arms around my body and curled into a ball, squeezing my knees into my chest for comfort. It took a long time to fall asleep that night.

The next morning we were awoken by a terrible stench.

It was putrid, sickening, the worst smell I'd ever smelled in my life.

'What the fuck is that?' Deborah screwed up her face in disgust.

I put my shirt up to my face. 'I don't know. I've never smelled anything like it. It's revolting!'

We were all reeling from the smell when Gary opened the door and came down with our breakfast – a couple of pieces of bread each.

The smell was stronger now – it was on his clothes, it hung in the air. I could even taste it in the bread. I stopped eating, fearing I might retch.

Nobody said much – we didn't ask him what the smell was. We didn't want to know.

In fact, we didn't know it at the time but the whole neighborhood was up in arms about the smell coming from Gary's house. They even called the cops, who banged on the front door. That was something we all heard. Of course we didn't know it was the cops. All we could hear was the banging on the door and Gary going to answer.

Officer Julio Aponte asked him what the smell was, telling him it was bothering his neighbors.

'I just burned my dinner,' Gary told him. And that was that – Officer Aponte was satisfied and went away. After all, you can't arrest a guy for being a bad cook. If he'd taken the trouble to investigate, however, he might have seen the four half-naked women chained in the basement and the real cause of the stench.

Once again, we were maddeningly close to rescue and yet nothing happened.

* * *

Three days later we discovered the cause of the horrendous smell.

Gary was downstairs beating up Deborah. He had her in the hole most of the time since she'd been here but she just wouldn't submit. Now she was refusing to get back down there and he was pounding on her ass but she just didn't seem bothered anymore.

'Is that the best you can do, jerk off?' she jeered.

Gary stopped. He threw the stick in a corner and went back upstairs. He came back with a key and unlocked her chain.

'Come upstairs with me,' he ordered. 'I've got something to show you.'

They were up there less than five minutes but when Deborah returned she looked terrified and she was shaking.

Gary rechained her and she went in the hole willingly.

We wanted to ask her what was wrong but she seemed so disturbed, we held off saying anything until later when she was let out again.

She was now sitting in the corner, her knees folded to her chest, her arms wrapped tightly round, rocking gently backward and forwards.

'Deborah, what's the matter? What happened up there?' asked Lisa.

Deborah just looked at us blankly, shaking her head. 'You don't want to know.'

'Come on,' I said. 'Tell us what happened.'

Deborah sighed and gave us a look, like, you asked for this, then started her horrific story.

'He took me upstairs and he showed me Sandra's head. It's sitting in a pot and he's boiling it on the stove. Then he showed me her ribs in a little roasting pan in the oven and he's got her arms and legs in the freezer.

'He says if I don't straighten up, that's going to be me soon.'

Jesus H Christ. He was cooking Sandra! My stomach turned over with the awful realization that the smell that had been coming out of his kitchen all this time was Sandra.

This was all getting too much. The others too were struck dumb with shock. My fingers were at my temples now, my breathing short and shallow. We all looked at each other, open-mouthed, none of us wanting to believe it, but knowing 100 per cent Deborah was telling the truth.

Deborah's hands covered her mouth, as if she regretted letting the words come out. That by telling us, by voicing what she had seen, it had become reality. She started to rock again.

Oh sweet Jesus, what next?

Chapter Twelve

Alpo

When I was little I was afraid of the dark.

My mom would usually let me fall asleep with the light on but at some point during the night she'd come into my room and switch it off.

A couple of times I'd wake up to complete blackness and scream the house down. 'Mom! Mom! It's dark in here. I don't like it. Turn on the lights!'

On one of these nights, Mom came bundling into my room. She wasn't mad but she wasn't going to let me have the light on again.

I'd be begging her to switch it on but she was adamant.

'What if you're in a situation where all the lights are out?' she asked me. 'You just have to adjust. Like there's day, there's night. That's part of life and something you're just going to have to get used to.'

'I can't,' I wailed.

'Yes you can!' she insisted. 'You just have to get used to it. Now quit your whining and go back to sleep.'

I was seven but you know what? I adjusted. I never slept with the light on after that. Mom didn't pander to my weaknesses. She understood them, she was sympathetic to them but at some point she was always firm at making me face my fears.

'Adjust. Get used to it,' those were her words.

And that's what I was trying to do in Gary's frightening new world. Trying to adjust. To get used to it.

It was mid-February now, though we wouldn't know this by the weather. We hadn't experienced anything of the outside world since our capture. All we had was the bare bulb over our heads, constantly glaring a harsh light in our faces, day and night.

Like there's day, there's night, my mom said, except in here there was no day and no night.

I missed the natural sunlight, the fresh air, rain, friends, family, freedom.

But I tried not to think about these things. I tried to adjust.

The other thing I wasn't thinking about was being pregnant. Aside from my periods disappearing, I had no other symptoms. Nothing. No nausea, my breasts weren't sore, and I wasn't displaying any of the signs that I had with my other pregnancies. Gary certainly didn't take any special care of me now that he thought I was pregnant either – it wasn't like he was giving me extra food or anything, and we never talked about it.

Every now and then Gary took us all upstairs for a bath. I let him watch me bathe in silence. I knew he thought about me now and I allowed him to think that I was on his side.

But the other girls, they were all trying their own thing too.

Jacqueline was chattering away the whole time he had her upstairs and when she got back he gave her two extra cookies.

'What's she getting cookies for?' Deborah demanded sullenly.

'Jackie here tells me what y'all are talking about while I'm not here,' Gary said.

'Jackie!' Lisa said, outraged.

But Jacqueline seemed oblivious. She wasn't trying to blab her mouth off for any reason – she was just the talkative type. I reckoned most of the time she didn't really know what was going on.

But it put me on edge.

I can't trust these other girls, I thought. *I don't know what they're telling him up there.*

Jacqueline was a pretty innocent girl, she was just being herself, but who's to say what she was talking about while he had her on his own?

I could tell Deborah was thinking the same thing because when he took her upstairs she tried talking to him too.

He brought her down but this time she didn't get any cookies.

'Hey, don't I get cookies too?' she shouted after him. 'I told you a whole load of shit.'

'Shut up, Deborah,' he sighed. 'I already heard all of that from Jacqueline. You gotta do better than that if you think that's enough to sort you out.'

Deborah started cursing him out again and he put her down in the hole as punishment.

She and Jacqueline spent most of their time in the hole now – for Jacqueline it was just because she was new and Gary was breaking her in. For Deborah, it was punishment. Always punishment.

Day after day Jacqueline and Deborah were stuck in that hole together and Deborah still didn't quit her yelling.

One night Lisa and me were trying to sleep and Deborah was still shouting her head off, so much so that we were exhausted listening to her. Every time I tried to think of my kids, hold their beautiful faces in my mind, she would scream and yell, shattering that picture into tiny pieces.

'Oh, will you please just *shut up*!' I shouted back for about the millionth time. I'd had it.

'Yeah, you better shut up!' Gary's deep voice behind me came as a shock and startled Lisa and me. We had no idea he was down here. He came in so quietly neither of us noticed.

'Jeez, you made me jump,' I said.

'We didn't realize you were down here,' Lisa added.

'I'm never far away,' he said darkly as he took up a stick once more and prepared to open the hole.

* * *

One day those girls were down in the hole and Gary was down in the basement with us when a dog food commercial came on the TV.

'Man, that Alpo looks good,' Deborah exclaimed loudly.

'Yeah,' Jacqueline laughed. 'I know what you mean.'

Deborah laughed too. 'Shit, that dog food looks too good

for them dogs. Look, it's got peas and vegetables in it and everything. Man, I could definitely have me some of that!'

I was playing cards with Lisa on the floor – Gary had given us a deck of cards and since Lisa and I were the ones usually up top with the other two in the hole, we wasted a lot of hours playing Rummy 500.

Now Lisa and I looked up at each other and started laughing.

'Oh really?' Gary said, putting his head to one side. 'You like the look of that dog food, huh?'

Oh for the love of God! Why don't you just keep your big mouth shut, Deborah?

This man didn't need any more sick ideas. He was doing pretty well on his own.

But sure enough, the next day he came down with an open can of dog food and a plastic fork. He opened the hole and leaned in, smiling wolfishly. Then he passed the can and fork to Deborah.

'Eat it!' he ordered.

She had no choice – she was the one who said it looked good in the first place and she even said she wouldn't mind having some.

Now she was spooning the lumpy gelatinous meat into her mouth. I expected her to throw up or recoil but it actually seemed like she was enjoying it.

Next Gary passed the can to Jacqueline and made her eat some too. She dug the fork in and pulled out a gristly greyish piece of meat.

'Hey, this don't have no peas in it,' she objected. 'This ain't Alpo – it's just some supermarket brand.'

'Eat it!' Gary ordered again. She knew better than to resist so she put the unappealing morsel in her mouth and chewed.

My face was screwed up in disgust. Lisa couldn't even look.

He made them eat the whole can – they seemed resigned. What could they do? They were hungry. And after that, Heidnik would regularly appear with a tin of dog food, and they'd eat it then, too.

All the while Lisa and I were exchanging fearful looks. We hoped he wouldn't make us eat it too. Luckily, we didn't agree with Deborah's thoughts about the dog food commercial in the first place so we got to stick with our normal diet.

And thank God for that – if any of us had known at the time what was really in that can, no one would have touched it.

* * *

I thought about my mom a lot.

I thought about the plate of lima beans we fought over when I was eight. She'd made me a tea of lima beans with fried chicken and potatoes. I ate all the chicken, I ate my potatoes but I refused the beans.

'What's for dessert?' I asked Mom, my elbows resting on the table, my legs kicking the air beneath me.

'Sit up straight, young lady,' she said, taking my plate away.

A minute later she set the same plate in front of me, complete with my rejected beans, this time with a desert spoon.

'For dessert, you've got lima beans!' she declared happily. I was outraged.

'Uh-uh,' I shook my head, pushing my chair away from the table and folding my arms in defiance. 'No way. I hate lima beans. There's no way I'm eating those.'

'Well, you're not getting anything till they're all gone.'

So we sat there like that for ages – it felt like hours – until finally Mom sighed. 'Okay, you can go to bed now.'

And I skipped up to bed, happy and confident I'd won the lima bean contest.

The next day, however, when I came down to breakfast, she set down the same plate in front of me. Those beans!

'Yuk!' I shouted. 'I'm not eating those damn beans.'

'Language!' Mom shot back. 'Like I said, you're not getting anything else until you finish them.'

I went to school that morning on an empty stomach and when I came back for lunch, I was met with that same damn plate of beans.

I realized with a heavy heart my mom wasn't kidding around – I wasn't getting any other food until I got rid of those beans! So, finally, in resignation, and after eighteen hours of refusing, I finally ate my beans.

It just goes to show, when you're hungry, you'll pretty much eat anything. I got used to lima beans and in the end I quite liked them. It was a mental shift, I guess. In order to get the lima beans down me the first time I told myself that I loved lima beans, that lima beans were my favorite thing in the whole world. And after that, I was fine. I adjusted.

* * *

But Deborah didn't adjust. She never quit planning and scheming.

One afternoon she and Jacqueline got let out of the hole and they popped up with sly smiles plastered all over their faces. After Gary had had sex with us all and returned upstairs, Jacqueline whispered to Lisa and me, 'We got a plan!'

Lisa wasn't impressed: 'Yeah? What's the plan?'

'You two can take him while we're in the hole and then you can let us out and we'll finish him off with the stick. Then we'll get out of here.'

'What about the keys?' Lisa asked the obvious question.

'You saw what happened to Sandra!' Deborah jumped in. 'You want that to happen to all of us? He doesn't give a damn if one or all of us die down here.'

Lisa looked thoughtful – Sandra's death had affected us all.

'What do you think, Nicole?' she asked me.

I sighed, exasperated. I felt like I was dealing with a kindergarten class. Ever since I'd got here and all these girls had been marched in one by one I'd decided one thing for certain: these girls didn't have much clue. I wanted to tell them I was working on Gary, that I had other ideas but the way they kept shooting their mouths off, I knew that it would be foolish and self-defeating.

'It's not going to work,' I said.

'Bullshit!' Deborah erupted at me. 'We don't know till we try. He might have the keys on him all along. You don't know for a fact what he's got in his pockets.'

'He's not that dumb,' I said. 'If he brought the keys down every time he knew it would be a risk to his whole plan. There are four of us. Of course he knows we could overcome him. You think he hasn't thought of that?

'What are we going to do afterwards? There are no tools down here, nothing we can use to open up the shackles and he's resealed the air vent. This place is a prison.'

'Never mind her.' Deborah waved her hand dismissively in my direction. 'She's been here too long now. She likes it down here. She and Gary got their own thing going on.'

'That's bullshit!' I denied vehemently.

'We can do this without you, Nicole!' Deborah blustered on. 'We don't need your fucking approval. Just keep quiet and I'll get us out of here. You can stay down here another year if you like.'

So they started plotting their moves, what they were going to do and when. But they'd forgotten to keep their voices down and like he said, Gary was never far away.

* * *

The next day I got taken up for a bath and Gary came right out with it. 'I hear you're planning to jump me in the basement.'

'I don't know about *we*, Gary, but yeah, there was a discussion about it,' I said, looking him straight in the eye.

He heard them talking about it but I tried to distance myself from the plan as far as possible.

Gary's eyes were boring into me now – I could see he was trying to assess how far I'd been involved.

'You know I don't carry the keys with me,' he said. 'So y'all would be stuck down there.'

'I know. I told them that.' I was trying to be as casual as possible. I just hoped he'd heard me earlier, telling them to lay off the plans.

'Look, you gotta expect them to try and think of ways to escape, Gary – that's just common sense,' I told him with confidence. 'You got them locked up here away from their families. It's natural they're gonna want to try and get out.

'You have to expect it. But that plan – that was just a dumb idea.'

Gary nodded thoughtfully – I could tell he was taking me seriously. And he'd heard me say 'they', like I was no longer one of them. At this point I was talking to him like a friend, not as one of the girls he had locked up.

Once we were downstairs again he said to the others, 'I know all about your little plan to try and jump me. And it wouldn't work. Even Nicole thinks it wouldn't work so you can put that thought right out of your heads. I don't carry the keys around with me. You'd all die down here without me.'

When he left Deborah ripped into me, her face contorted with fury. 'You told him, you rat! How could you tell him about the plan? I knew you weren't to be trusted.'

'He heard you! I didn't have to say anything. You weren't smart enough even to keep your voices down while you were discussing it.'

'You could have lied,' Lisa was mad at me too. 'You could have told him it wasn't true.'

'Hey, nobody's stopping you doing it, even if he knows about the goddamn plan,' I spat back. 'If all you three think it's such a great idea go ahead – kill the man who is keeping us alive!'

* * *

That night I thought of Mom again, of the day she taught me how to ride a bike.

I was six years old and all the other kids my age had training wheels on their bikes, helping to keep them upright, their parents scared in case they fell over and hurt themselves.

And when my dad brought one of my foster sister's bikes out of the garage there were training wheels on it too.

'She don't need those!' said Mom and she took them off.

I was fearful – how am I going to stay on if I don't have the little wheels at the back for balance?

But Mom just waved away my worries.

'Just get on the bike and balance yourself,' she instructed as I climbed on the red bike and wobbled uncertainly.

'You can do this,' Mom said encouragingly. 'I'm going to hold the back for you while you push the pedals. The faster you go, the more chance you've got of staying up. So just push and keep on pushing.'

So then we started. I fell a couple of times but Mom never treated me like a baby.

'Get back up,' she said firmly. 'You're only gonna learn by falling off a few times.'

So I quickly wiped the tears away and in under half an hour I was riding my bike round the park like a pro.

I was six years old and all the rest of the kids on the block still had their training wheels on for another year. Mom was prepared for me to fall but she knew I would quickly learn how to stay steady.

She trusted me, you see. And she knew I was only going to get better by falling.

I felt so different from all the other kids who were still pedaling around with their little wheels – I felt bigger, older, smarter.

And that's how I felt now.

Bigger, older and smarter than these other girls – I was in a situation I wasn't prepared for, learning to adapt, to find a way through and not fall.

Chapter Thirteen
Sleepless

In the quiet early hours of the morning Lisa nudged me awake. I think it must have been early March. Springtime. The outside world would be going through that yearly stage of renewal, but there seemed to be no such renewal for us, no such hope. I had a new life I was carrying inside me, but not one I wanted. Luckily I didn't have a bump to constantly remind me I was pregnant.

'Hey Nicole. Nicole? You sleeping?' Her voice punctured the fog of unconsciousness like a siren, tugging me out of a restless sleep.

My dreams were frightening these days, clouded by dark ominous shapes that I couldn't ever seem to see clearly. It wasn't really like sleep at all. It was more a passive form of watchfulness, where half of my being rested while the other half stayed wide awake, just in case, just in case...

I opened my eyes slowly, shielding them from the light with my hand. It was a practice I had become used to since falling asleep in this strange light.

Lisa crouched next to me, her arms wrapped around herself, fear and loneliness seeping from her eyes.

'Can't sleep, huh?' I asked her gently.

She shook her head.

She needed comfort, just to hear the sound of another person's voice – I knew the feeling.

'Tell me about your home, your mom and dad,' she pleaded, a little girl needing a story before bedtime.

I wasn't feeling particularly talkative but I was as keen as her to chase the demons from my mind so I started to talk.

And the more I did, the more I enjoyed it. It felt good to tell her about my childhood and the people I loved in the world – it reminded me that they were still out there somewhere and gave me hope that I'd be reunited with them.

I told her about Mom and Althea, about my Catholic school and all the brothers and sisters who were often at our house.

'What about your dad?' she asked.

'What about him?'

'You don't talk about him much.'

'There isn't an awful lot to say. For me, it was always Mom. We were with her night and day. Besides, by the time I came along my dad was retired and as a kid I just remember he spent the majority of his time upstairs in his room.

'My parents slept in separate bedrooms – he was on the third floor and she was on the second so I didn't see him an awful lot. Then as I got older I noticed he wasn't remembering stuff very well. He became more and more closed off from everybody in the house except for at mealtimes. He was a lot older than my mom and she became his carer as he started to go downhill.

'He was slowly losing his ever-loving mind but Mom, she was amazing. He couldn't walk in the end so we had a hospital bed in our home. We had to change him and wash him and feed him. Me and Mom, we took care of him together.

'My mom liked having things to do so she kept herself busy.

'Dad wouldn't talk at all now – the only person he ever had words for was the priest. That used to rile my mom. The priest would come and pray with him and whenever he walked in he'd say, "Mr Patterson, how are you?"

And my dad would say, "I'm all right."

So then Mom would say, "Oh now you can talk! But when we ask you stuff you don't say anything!" Yeah, that really riled her.

'He died at home and Mom was prepared for it. He was ready to go by then, he had a tube in his stomach and Mom had nursed him right through to the end. I was only fourteen.'

I didn't tell her about my birth father, the one I found at sixteen. Me and Iris had been talking for a time about trying to track down our birth parents.

We wanted to know who they were, where they came from and whether we had brothers and sisters.

We started at the records office where we found the original social security reports on how they found us kids. In the papers it stated the apartment was filthy and freezing cold and I was in a wet bed wearing just a T-shirt and a nappy soaked through with urine. My sister was so malnourished she couldn't walk.

Seeing it in black and white like that was strange – I'd known about the circumstances of how I was found since I was twelve when my mom had told me. But reading it in the files was different. I couldn't see myself as one of those children, I felt so removed from it all. All I could think was 'those poor kids', as if they were someone else's family.

I wasn't angry, I just wanted to know – how had they ended up like that? What drove my parents away?

The records left a paper trail with my father's name and his last recorded address – Porfirio Rivera. I learned that Porfirio was an alcoholic so he hadn't given the authorities a lot of clear information on either himself or my mother Maria.

They'd lived in New York initially then they'd come to Philadelphia, where they married and where I was born. According to the records, they were no longer together.

At least for my dad there was a birth date and previous addresses – for my mom, there was nothing. So if we were to have any kind of hope of finding her, we needed to find him first.

We went through so many agencies, filling out forms, giving them proof of our identities. Finally, I wound up in the state building in Philadelphia where a kind but busy man who clearly had better things to do with his time told me that if I could bring in my birth certificate, he'd see what he could do to help.

I returned the next day. After checking my documents the man told me straight out: 'Your father is living at 929 North Sixth Street and if he's not there when you get there let us know because we will cut his check off. This is where he is supposed to be living and even if you don't get him there, don't worry, we will find your father.'

In the end, I went to see my dad with a friend with instructions from Iris to call her if it turned out to be the right man. I was nervous, of course I was, but I was also determined to know the truth. I wasn't angry or upset – I truly believed that they'd done me a favor because I ended up with a wonderful family.

No, it wasn't about retribution. Things happen; I understand that. I just wanted to know who I was related to.

We took the trolley to North Sixth Street, a road in a good neighborhood called Northern Liberties. By the time we'd walked the length of the street to 929, my heart was in my mouth. But I didn't think for a second of going back. It only took a few seconds before a man came to the door, a man who looked exactly like me: large full lips, high cheekbones and a small straight nose. But you could tell from the deep lines on his face and soft saggy eyes that his had not been an easy life.

The shock of seeing someone who looked so familiar and yet was still a stranger was almost too much for me and I had trouble getting my words out. I'd planned my speech so carefully but in that moment it all flew out of my head. Now I was stumbling and stuttering and trying hard just to remember my own name!

'Erm, excuse me, ahem. My name is Josefina Rivera,' I started. 'I've been given your address because I think you might be my father.'

That's all I said and he started to cry – if there was ever any doubt before that this man was my father, it was wiped out in that instant.

He knew it was true, he could see it for myself.

Porfirio told me all about the family – there were seventeen children altogether, including four sets of twins. My dad had six kids before he married my mom and she already had four before she met him.

And they had both had kids since we were all taken. Of all of us, she kept Ada, her firstborn, with her. She left us, the babies.

'Why did you abandon us?' I wanted to know.

My dad started crying again.

'I had to make a life for myself,' is all he would say.

I stayed with my dad a couple of hours that day and Iris came down later on. I went back again and again to see him, to learn as much as I could about my family. But I never did find Maria – nobody seemed to know what had happened to her. She just disappeared into thin air.

Soon after Iris got a house on North Sixth Street and I wound up spending a lot of time at my father's house. By now he had remarried a woman called Anne Mae and his wife had two sons of her own. One of them was Robert, Ricky and Zornae's father.

Dad was a storyteller – he loved to recount the times from his past long ago in Puerto Rico. He'd moved to New York after a bad monsoon season and he still didn't know where his parents were after that devastating event.

I loved to listen to him talk and talk but every time I asked him about my mom, his memory failed.

My foster mom understood my desire to get closer to my real dad – but that didn't mean she approved. She got the measure of him all those years ago when he came to visit the house.

The fact was, Dad was a functioning yet utterly hopeless alcoholic. From the moment he got up in the morning till the last thing at night he drank Thunderbirds, a fruit-flavored fortified wine that he bought by the gallon at the convenience store. He'd been drinking since he was thirteen and to be honest, if he'd stopped, I don't think he would have lasted very long. Being with him just made me grateful I'd found a secure and loving home with my foster mom.

* * *

At some point I must have dozed off because I was brought back to the present by hollering and banging coming from the hole.

For Christ's sake – we couldn't get a moment's peace!

Ten minutes later Gary was downstairs with us.

'Everything okay?' he asked.

'Them girls down there are getting on our nerves,' I said. 'They won't shut up.'

'I couldn't hear them,' he said, puzzled.

So then he went back upstairs and conducted a little experiment. He took his car out of the garage and they started hollering and banging again.

They could hear the vibrations of the car when he took it out and they figured he was out of the house so they could make as much noise as they liked.

He tiptoed back into the house and stood at the basement door, listening to the noise.

Then he pulled his car back into the garage and because they heard him coming back, they figured he was in the house and they shut up. So he came back down to the basement and realized they knew he must be back again.

So the next time he came down it was with the screwdrivers. He got Jacqueline and Deborah out of the hole and he put the screwdrivers in their ears, just like he did with me and Sandra.

If only that had been the worst of it. If only things hadn't gone any further. Years later I looked back and wondered if things could have gone another way. Maybe if Deborah had submitted to Gary, just given in, he wouldn't have thought of all these other forms of punishment.

Maybe. But then maybe he was so far gone at this point it was inevitable there would be another tragedy.

I don't know. All I knew was that Gary's next idea had devastating consequences for all of us. And perversely, it marked the start of the end of my incarceration.

Chapter Fourteen

Losing Deborah

It was a week later when Gary came downstairs holding a wire and a hose.

He lifted the board off the hole and he handcuffed Jacqueline and Deborah together. Then he got the hose and fitted it to a nearby faucet before filling the hole up with cold water. We all just watched him in silence, wondering what the hell he had planned.

When the water was a few inches deep, he turned it off and replaced the board over the top of the hole. Then he picked up the wire, which looked like an ordinary extension cord, except on one end he'd cut it down so that the insulation plastic was gone and the bare wires exposed.

He plugged the other end into a socket and now we all knew what was coming. He was going to electrocute the girls in the hole.

Realizing what was happening, Jacqueline and Deborah begged Gary not to do it but he was completely intent on his task.

'Don't worry,' he said coolly. 'The current isn't that strong. It's just a little shock. Nothing too bad. I just got to get you both to straighten up a little.'

'No, don't do it!' Deborah shrieked.

'Please, please, please,' Jacqueline screamed, sobbing.

He touched the bare wires to the girls' chains, which were sticking out of a gap in the board, and violent screams erupted from the hole accompanied by the sound of struggling. My heart lurched.

He held it there for a few seconds before taking the wire off. Then he waited as he listened to the sounds coming from the hole. They were panting hard and crying. He seemed satisfied.

'Okay, now you do it.' He turned to me. Oh God, no! *NO*! I really did not want to do this. I felt sick, desperate. I wanted to run but I had no choice – I knew that if I didn't comply it would be me down in that hole next.

So I took the wires, trying to still my shaking hands, and held them to the chains. The girls screamed again.

The yelling and splashing coming from the hole told us the punishment was effective. Lisa and I couldn't look at each other.

'Now, just you both think about that awhile,' he called into the hole as he took the wire out of the socket and returned upstairs.

'Are you both okay?' I put my head close to the hole so they could hear me whisper.

'Shit!' Deborah exclaimed. 'Shit shit *shit*! That bastard is trying to kill us!'

'Was it terrible?' Lisa asked.

'It wasn't nice!' retorted Jacqueline. 'But it wasn't like, you know, a big jolt. I thought it would be worse. It was more the anticipation of knowing what was coming. We could see through the holes in the board what he was doing and I was scared as hell.'

'This sure is a fucked-up way to make babies!' Deborah spat.

'Yeah.' Lisa sat back on her heels. Gary's mind was leading him down some very dark alleys and he was taking us all with him.

* * *

Two days later he had the girls sitting in a puddle of water again.

We went through the same routine – first Gary put the wire to the chain and then it was my turn.

Deborah and Jacqueline were screaming and struggling again.

After a while he went upstairs and silence took over.

He was up there a good ten minutes before Jacqueline yelled: 'Deborah's dead.'

Me and Lisa looked at each other, aghast, unable, unwilling to move.

Is she serious? I can't believe it. What do we do now?

None of us moved or spoke but when Gary returned I told him: 'Jackie says Deborah's dead.'

'Is she?'

'I don't know.'

Gary moved over to the hole and lifted up the board. The girls were both sitting with their legs straight out in front of them, wrists meeting where they were cuffed, but Deborah's legs were spread apart and her body had fallen forwards so that she was lying with her face in the water. For the first time since I'd known her, she was still.

Gary pulled her up by her hair and it was clear she was gone – the rivulets of water dripped down her blank face, her eyes and mouth fell open in a slack, silent scream.

He uncuffed her from Jacqueline who jumped out of the hole like she'd been stung. Then he pulled Deborah out and laid her on the floor.

'Thank God for that!' he said. 'Now all my problems are over and my basement can get back to normal.'

We all looked at each other. It wasn't like with Sandra. Nobody cried, we were all too stunned. Gary went back up the stairs.

'How did she die?' Lisa wondered.

Jacqueline just shrugged. I couldn't work it out myself. If the shocks weren't too bad, what killed her? Maybe she had a heart attack. Maybe her body couldn't handle the lack of food and constant confinement in an enclosed place as well as the electric shocks.

Jacqueline was trembling now and Lisa put a comforting arm around her.

Gary quickly returned with the keys to Deborah's chains and when he got them off her he took her body upstairs in a fireman's lift.

Ten minutes later he was back downstairs again. This time he had a piece of paper and a pen.

He handed them to me and instructed: 'Put the date at the top. March 18, 1987.'

I did as I was told.

'Now the time – it's 6.30 p.m. Okay, now write this: "I, Nicole Rivera, and Gary Heidnik killed Deborah Dudley by applying electricity to her chain while sitting in a pool of water in a hole in the basement of 3520 North Marshall Street." Now sign it.'

I followed his instructions without question – what did this all mean? When I was done he got Lisa and Jacqueline to sign the paper as witnesses.

'Now I've got this letter,' – he held it up for me to see – 'if you ever go to the cops, I can use this as evidence that you killed Debbie.'

My mind was whirring, buzzing from the shock but also trying desperately to keep up with the rapidly changing situation. He thought I was guilty of killing Deborah.

He thought I was as guilty as he was.

Next he bent down and undid the shackles around my ankles.

'Now go upstairs and get into bed.'

I could hardly believe it. In the act of torturing Deborah to death, I was rewarded with my freedom. It was grotesque.

It was what I've been working towards this whole time and yet in order to get it, one of us had to die.

I didn't say a word. What was there to say?

I turned my back on the girls downstairs and I walked up, towards my freedom. To the outside world.

I could hardly let myself believe it was true – *this could all be a trick*, I was thinking.

He could be testing me. Don't screw this up, Josefina! I told myself. *Hold tight, hold tight – you only get one shot at this and if it doesn't work it could all be over.*

I was standing now in the first floor of Gary's house, looking about at the rooms I walked through four months before. Nothing had changed and yet in that time everything in my world had altered, perhaps for ever.

Two girls were dead. I'd been starved, beaten, raped, tortured and transformed into an accomplice of a man whose evil knew no limits.

I wanted to run back down and tell her, 'Don't worry. I'm going to find a safe way out of this for all of us. I'm going to get us all out.'

But I couldn't – I couldn't let him see my mask slip for a minute. I was now Josefina, accomplice and killer. He could only see what he wanted to see – everything else was sentimentality. And sentimentality could get us all killed.

I worked my way up the dark staircase towards the bedroom – for the first time in four months my feet were unencumbered by chains.

I felt so light I was afraid I might float away. Every step felt like an ascent away from the darkness, away from the depths of hell.

I was free. *Free*! It was all over for me, I knew that. I knew I only had to ask him now and Gary would let me out of the house, safe in the knowledge that he 'had' me. I was on his side. Even if I ran I wouldn't tell the police because I was as implicated as him. That was his assessment of our situation.

He was coming up behind me now but I didn't falter for a minute. I just kept right on walking, I didn't turn round or stop to talk to him.

He had to think this is what I wanted too – so I walked into his bedroom, slipped under the sheets of his sloping bed and I turned on my side towards the window.

I needed time to think, time to let it all sink in.

I could run now, if I wanted to, except there were still two girls chained up in that basement. And if I made a break for my freedom, there was really only one course of action for him. He had to kill them.

So now I had to find a way out for all of us.

It was some time later before Gary climbed into bed next to me. He didn't try to have sex with me. He just turned the light off and went to sleep.

I lay awake the whole night, thinking about Deborah, thinking about the arguments we'd had.

I heard her voice: 'I'm going to die here, aren't I?'

Then mine: 'Yeah, pretty much.'

I'm sorry Deborah, I'm so so sorry.

Chapter Fifteen

Upstairs

The sun rose on a new reality. At some point in the night exhaustion took over and, combined with the fact that I was lying in a bed in the dark for the first time in four months, I'd fallen asleep.

Now the early spring sunlight peeked through the curtains and I felt elated at that tiny glimpse into the outside world. Sunlight! I wanted to get up and run out of the house that very minute but I knew it wasn't that simple. As much as I needed to get back to my children, to see them again, I couldn't do that to Lisa and Jacqueline.

The man lying next to me was a cold-hearted killer. The man lying next to me wouldn't hesitate to kill the two women downstairs if he suspected I was going to turn him in. So now I was playing a role and I had to do it perfectly. I slipped quietly out of bed and went next door to the bathroom to run myself a bath. As I waited for the tub to fill, I looked around. It was a small bathroom – a razor and shaving foam on one side of the sill, toothbrush and paste on the other.

I picked up Gary's toothpaste and squeezed a little onto the tip of my finger. Then I put my finger in my mouth and worked the minty paste around my gums and teeth. It tasted so good – my first taste of toothpaste in four months. I didn't want to use his toothbrush. I wasn't sure yet just how free I was.

I got in the warm tub and scrubbed myself over and over again, then when I got out I wrapped a towel around me and walked from room to room in search of some clothes.

I peered into the spare room – just junk, old TVs, sofas, chairs, nothing I could wear. I returned to the bedroom where Gary was now sitting up in bed, pulling a shirt over his vest.

'What can I wear?' I asked him.

He got up slowly and went to the dresser where he pulled out a shirt and a black pair of his jeans.

'Put these on for now,' he said. 'We'll get you some stuff soon.'

I pulled on the jeans – they were massive so I took a belt hanging off the chair and pulled it tight round my waist, rolling up the legs at the bottom so I didn't stand on the ends.

He went downstairs and I followed him. He prepared a pot of coffee then grabbed some slices of white bread out of a bag on the counter – breakfast for Lisa and Jacqueline. I took a slice myself and ate it standing up.

I didn't want to go downstairs to the basement with him – I couldn't face those girls.

While he was gone I looked about me – it was just an ordinary kitchen. There was cereal on the counter, tea and a coffee pot, a food processor and a collection of snacks and tins in the cupboard: crackers, soup, dog food, packets of noodles.

When he returned he made us a cup of coffee each then after about ten minutes, he started talking. It was almost like he was talking aloud to himself.

'Deborah – we got to find somewhere to dump Deborah,' he started thoughtfully.

I looked about me.

'Where *is* Deborah?'

'I wrapped her up and put her in the freezer last night. Now Sandra, I had a whole lot of trouble with her. Folks knew she was with me, you see? I couldn't just dump her body or they'd come looking for me. So I had to think of other ways.'

Jesus Christ, I thought. I had a horrible feeling what these 'other ways' might be, from what he had showed Deborah all those weeks ago.

He walked towards a large pot sitting on the stove and lifted the lid, then beckoned me over to show me. The smell hit me instantly. Deborah had told me what to expect, but still, the horror of it was worse than I could imagine.

Inside the scorched aluminum pot was a bare white skull sitting in a pool of brown-yellow liquid. It was so stark, so ugly. The pale shiny bone almost seemed to glow against the putrid dark water.

'I cooked her head,' he explained matter-of-factly. 'And then I put her ribs in the oven and roasted them, like this, see?'

My stomach flipped over. Acidic bile rose in the back of my throat but on the outside, I was calm, placid. I had to be. He yanked open the fridge door and reached inside. He pulled out a roasting pan with the unmistakable burnt remains of a human ribcage. It had been well over a month since Deborah had told us of what she had seen, and here were the ribs she had described, charred and what little flesh there was on them rotting away.

Sandra's ribs.

Sandra.

My head swam, my guts heaved. His voice was coming to me in waves, the sound rippling in and out, and I felt I might pass out. I grabbed onto the counter for support, but Gary didn't notice my alarm. He just kept right on talking.

'I had to put this in the fridge because it was smelling real bad and there were complaints from the neighbors.

'I've got some other bits in the freezer here.' He opened up the freezer part of the fridge and inside, stacked from top to bottom were neat little packages of meat, just like on a butcher's counter.

The first package he picked up was her forearm. He showed it to me as he was talking.

'So I had this idea that I would take the meat off and then feed the bones to the neighborhood dogs. But the dogs didn't bury the bones or take them away. I kept looking out into the yard and seeing giant pieces of hip bones out there, which wasn't any good. Because at some point somebody might see these things and realize they're not normal bones.'

I was reeling. The thought of Sandra being there in that

kitchen in little bits and stuffed in bags was too much. But things were about to get even worse.

'So then it's Deborah who sets off the whole thing with the dog food.'

'The dog food?' I tried to disguise my disgust, to keep my voice cool and level but it was so hard. Everything he was telling me and showing me was beyond belief.

'Yeah, you know she said she wanted to eat dog food. So I got a few cans and then I minced up some of Sandra's body and mixed that with the dog food and put it back in the cans so they wouldn't know. That's what they were eating. I figure eventually they'll eat the whole of Sandra and I don't have to worry anymore. I got the idea from a film, *Eating Raoul*. It's a good film. I'll show it to you sometime.'

My mind went back to all the times down in the basement when he fed Deborah and Jacqueline with dog food; their forks digging into the soft chunks of meat, Jacqueline complaining about the lack of peas.

It was too much.

I tried to focus on Gary and what he was saying.

I needed to pull myself together.

He was recounting all of this like it was normal. *None of this is normal*, I wanted to scream. *You've killed two women and now you're feeding them to other people? This is fucked up. Strike that. This is beyond fucked up. I have no words for what this is.*

'Nobody knew Deborah was here with me,' he was saying, taking deep, long slurps of his coffee. 'So that means we can go right out and find a place to dump her body and just so long as it's not too obvious, there's no reason the cops will link it back here.'

Now I noticed that he talked about 'we' all the time – this meant that whatever he was doing I was doing too.

I wanted to cry. I wanted to curl up in a corner and weep for the awful, unnatural things this lunatic had done. But all I could do was keep hold of the counter to steady me and nod as Gary talked.

'I think I know a place we can go. It's right over in the Pine Barrens. But we have to be careful. We can't stop at any tollbooths or nothing, got to make sure we've got the right change. We'll go and find a place first then we'll come back and get the body.'

He sauntered into the living room and I realized then that I'd been holding my breath. Not wishing to spend another second in that kitchen, I followed him, letting myself exhale silently as I did so.

He threw me a stained cream sweater and I put it on. It smelled of him.

'I don't have to tell you about the letter again, do I?'

It was less of a question, more of a threat.

I shook my head and gave him a look, like, are you kidding me?

He disappeared upstairs for a short time and that was when I took a good look around – all the windows had bars on them, the doors were fitted with two-way locks so I couldn't get out without a key and I couldn't see a phone anywhere.

When he got back down again he was holding a worn and battered pair of sneakers – it looked like they'd come from a thrift store.

I put them on silently. I couldn't imagine how I looked – an oversized jumper, jeans falling off me and my hair a state.

But my looks were the last thing that mattered to me right now. I was about to step outside for the first time in months.

Gary took the front door key out his pocket to let us out but I noticed it didn't look right. The tip part was missing.

'What's wrong with your key?' I said.

'Nothing, I made it that way,' he answered proudly. 'I put the regular key halfway in and sawed it off. The front half stays permanently in the lock.'

'Why'd you do that?'

'So no other key except mine will work.'

Made sense.

Bizarrely, and not for the first time, I marveled at how such a clearly intelligent man could be so wholly lacking in humanity. He was smart in a terrifying way because that thing that marks us out as humans, a natural sense of right and wrong, an instinctive aversion to pain and suffering, was missing from him.

Underneath the surface, there was nothing: no emotion, no sympathy, no understanding. He was like a robot walking round in a human suit. And that was what made him so dangerous. If you looked at him you'd never imagine for a minute he was any different from you. Until you've met someone like Gary you can't even imagine another human acting this way. Then, when you have, you realize that everything you thought you knew could be false. How many other Garys were out there? The thought was terrifying.

The door swung open and I felt a rush of air hit me full in the face. It was amazing.

Fresh air!

Cold, clean air! It filled my nostrils then my mouth, throat and lungs. I was drinking it down like water. For a moment I forgot about Gary and just stood there, letting the sunlight warm my skin and the wind blow through my hair. But I couldn't hang about – already Gary was moving towards the garage and I followed him.

I looked up and down the street. The neighborhood was poor, dirty and downtrodden. I knew I could run away but what would happen then? He'd just go right back in the house and kill the other two girls.

Then he'd deny it all.

One time when me and Sandra were in the basement he boasted to us: 'I won't ever get sent down. I'm crazy, you see? If they catch me and take me to court I'll just stand right up and salute everybody.'

He'd laughed mirthlessly.

'I can beat those stupid psychiatric tests they set me. I know them inside and out. They'll just keep sending me round the different hospitals while I keep collecting my checks. By the time they figure out what's wrong with me I'll be gone again.'

No, I didn't have a hope of getting the girls out as long

as he was around. My mind was ticking over, trying to take as much in as possible.

We went into his garage now and I saw the Rolls-Royce he had next to the Cadillac. He climbed into the Cadillac and opened the door up so I could get in next to him. Then we took off and we drove through the city in broad daylight.

Josefina Rivera and Gary Heidnik.

We drove east, right across the city, over the Delaware River by the Ben Franklin Bridge and into New Jersey. It was astonishing to see other people on the sidewalk and in their cars – I couldn't stop staring, wondering about each person, what they were doing, where they were going and who they were going to meet. I felt so separate from the world now, like I didn't belong in it at all. I was just a visitor, let out for the day, to gawp at the ordinary folk in their ordinary lives.

The journey took about an hour and on the way we stopped at an off-road diner where Gary got himself a burger and fries.

I sat in the booth opposite him, sipping on a Coke while he demolished his food.

I was around people for the first time in months. It was bizarre.

I envied them, all just going about their normal lives, nothing to worry about except what to cook for their dinner or their plans for the weekend.

It seemed so far removed from my existence. I felt like I'd been pushed into a different plane of reality where daily horrors were the norm, where people died and got minced up into dog food.

I watched Gary as he ate – he didn't seem to have a care in the world.

'More coffee, honey?' The waitress was a weathered old broad with peroxide hair and a world-weary expression.

'Fill her up.' Gary pushed his cup in her direction and she poured him a cup to the top.

'You want anything?' she asked me.

'No, I'm okay,' I replied, too scared to ask for anything. In fact, I didn't even want to look at her, just in case Gary read something into my expression that angered him or made him suspect me.

It didn't even occur to me to try and scream or run out. It would have been too risky.

After another half an hour we were driving along Route 676 in the densely forested Pine Barrens. It all looked the same, mile after mile of pine forest, nothing to distinguish one place from the next, when suddenly Gary pulled the car off the road and down a tiny track that led into the forest.

If you'd never been there before you might just drive right by, never knowing it was there at all. There was no sign, no road marking or landmark to tell you where you were. Just a very small dirt track leading into the woods. After a couple of hundred yards, Gary stopped the car and turned the engine off.

He got out, looked around a bit before getting back in the car.

'This'll do,' he said.

Then we drove home.

Chapter Sixteen
The Pine Barrens

By the time we got back to the house it was mid-afternoon. Gary put the coffee on again and I turned on the TV in the living room.

I let my mind go blank as the game shows blurred into commercial breaks. Minutes slid into hours and I just sat there, too worn out and exhausted to move. Just a couple of times, I got up to go to the bathroom and get a glass of water.

Mainly, I just sat there, lost in my own thoughts. I wondered about the drugs Gary was on and whether he was taking them. I wondered about the drugs he said the army had given him all those years ago. Could the drugs have made him do the things he did or was he born that way? How do you lose all your morality? How do you go about killing people as if it's just an everyday thing? It was bizarre to me that he had reacted so indifferently to Sandra and Deborah's deaths given how he'd outlined his plans to us to build a harem of women and children in his home. He wanted to create life – surely, killing us wasn't part of the plan. Did he care? It occurred to me that maybe I wasn't the first one there. Maybe he'd got another woman or women before me and he'd ended up killing them just like Sandra and Deborah. Was I really the first or was I a replacement? I didn't have a clue, I just had to take this guy at his word. For all I knew he'd dumped a dozen bodies in the Pine Barrens already. He sure knew his way to some out-of-the-way parts of the woods without a map! What if he ended up killing all of us? Gary's plans were coming apart at the seams but he didn't seem to notice, or care. He went along with every new development like abducting young women and murdering them was just a part of life. Every way I looked at it my situation was terrifying – if he'd never killed before he didn't seem to have any feeling about doing it for the first time and if he had killed before then who knew who would be next?

I could hear him moving around the house, sifting through post and papers, clearing cups and plates from the dining room table.

Once he returned to the basement and he was down there some time so I figured he must be having sex with the other girls. He was still sticking to his plan of getting them pregnant, but now that he thought I was, he didn't bother with me. The thought of having his baby was so repugnant to me that I just put it to one side. I knew that if it came to that, I would get rid of it. Besides, I had much more urgent things to think about – like finding a means for us all to escape.

It was night time when he returned to the living room and looked at me. 'Come on.'

He opened the door to the basement and disappeared downstairs but this time he returned with Deborah's frozen body bent double in a clear trash bag. I turned away.

'Look at her!' he commanded. I didn't want to. First I had to see her die, then I had to see Sandra in pieces and now he wanted me to look at Deborah in a bag? It was one more horrific image I didn't need permanently lodged in my mind. But I really didn't have any choice.

So I turned back. There she was, her taut skin frozen solid over her bones, her body folded perfectly in half. Mercifully, her head was tucked between her legs so her face was hidden by her hair.

'Now, get in the car,' he ordered. There was no anger in his voice, no emotion at all.

I went outside and got in the passenger side of the car. Behind me I heard a click as he opened up the trunk, then I heard a heavy thunk as her body hit the back of the car. The trunk door slammed shut, then he got in beside me.

Now we were driving back across the city, over the Ben Franklin Bridge and out into the Pine Barrens again.

The lights flickered past, the billboards screamed out their enthusiastic slogans. I just hunched myself into the side door and settled in for the long journey.

* * *

It must have been late by the time we reached the same dirt track we found earlier in the day – there weren't many cars on the road, most of the diners were shut.

Gary pulled slowly into the forest then he stopped the car, got out and I heard the trunk catch open. I didn't move.

Next I felt another whump from the back of the car as

her body hit the trunk again – I reckoned he must have taken her out of the bag.

There was a snapping and crunching sound as he moved through the twigs and leaves on the forest floor before I saw him walk round the side of the car with Deborah in his arms, still neatly folded in two. He strode into the woods where there was a little opening and I could hear my breath now coming in short little pants.

It was completely black out there, completely silent.

Remember this, I told myself. *Remember this place.*

If I ever got out of this alive I knew someone was going to want to come back here to retrieve Deborah so I was trying desperately to make an imprint of the place onto my mind.

But all the while, I was gripped with fear.

What if he decided to dump me out here with her? Nobody knew we were here. They'd never find me. I was paralyzed, sick with terror.

In the oppressive darkness of the forest, my paranoia took over. He could just kill me out here and no one would know. What would I do? How would I get away?

I looked about wildly around the inside of the car but I couldn't see anything I could use as a weapon. He'd taken the car keys with him so I couldn't just drive away. The only course open to me would be to run into the woods and pray he wouldn't find me. Then I'd be all alone in the woods in the dark, shivering, terrified and alone.

He wasn't gone longer than three minutes but it felt like an hour.

To my great relief he just slammed the trunk door shut and got into the car next to me. He didn't say a word.

We reversed out of the drive and headed back towards Philadelphia.

On the way back we stopped at a gas station to pick up a copy of the *Philadelphia Inquirer*.

'To check my stocks,' Gary explained as he chucked it down on the back seat.

He pulled up at 52nd and Walnut – a bright, sleazy part of town that seemed to come alive in the early hours, a lot of strip malls and fast food joints.

We turned into a McDonald's and I realized we were getting out for another food stop.

As we walked into the restaurant, he threw something into the trash can – it was the bag that he used to carry Deborah's body.

The light and sound hit me like a train as I walked in – the place was crowded, really crowded. People were all around me, they shoved and jostled as we all stood in line, those with trays elbowed their way past to the seats.

There was shouting, laughter, chatter and a heft of people so great I could hardly catch my breath.

I looked about in wonder. Did these people realize what we'd just done?

We just dumped a dead body in the woods and here they all were, acting like nothing was wrong.

I was wretched.

Gary got himself another burger and fries, this time with

a milkshake. He asked me if I wanted anything. No, I shook my head dumbly.

Then he picked out a table in the corner and we sat down. It was all I could do to stop my whole body from trembling but Gary was just calmly eating his dinner as if nothing had happened.

He propped the paper open on his leg and concentrated hard on the pages as he devoured bite after bite of the soft, doughy bun, occasionally, absent-mindedly letting his hands wander onto the tray in front of him to grasp a fistful of fries.

'Looks like my Crazy Eddie stocks are still low,' he mumbled, shaking his head. 'Damn, I sure got caught on that one. I'm down $16,000.'

The whole scene was surreal, unbelievable. If somebody had told me six months before I'd be dumping a body in New Jersey before stopping at a McDonald's, I'd never have believed it. Now it was happening and I still couldn't believe it.

My nerves were shot. I ached with the effort of trying to appear normal. I had one elbow resting on the table, supporting my head with my knuckles. My other hand was clamped between my crossed legs. I was wound as tight as a drum and yet I knew if I didn't pull this off, this act of seeming relaxed, I could be dead tomorrow.

Gary's reactions were so abnormal, so out of my realm of experience, it took me a while for the penny to drop. Suddenly, I saw things very clearly – he'd been acting as if this was all normal for months!

In order to succeed to this point, he'd had to go about his business in the world like nothing was wrong, all while he had us all chained up in his basement.

'I can fool anyone,' was his boast to me and Sandra. 'They think they know what crazy looks like so I show them the crazy they want to see. That's the point – people can only see what you show them. If you don't let on, how are they to know what's really going on?'

So now he acted like a regular guy because he knew what a regular guy looked like. He showed the world what it wanted to see – he kept the real crazy hidden.

I've got to do the same, I realized it now. *I've got to show him what he wants to see, nothing more.*

The sounds and the stirrings of the people around us faded into the background. It was just me and Gary.

I looked at him, slurping his milkshake and scanning the paper.

Have you done this before? I wondered. *You sure as hell knew what to do with a body. You killed two girls damn near back to back and you didn't blink an eye.*

Surely, the first time you kill someone there's a reaction, whoever you are.

Are there more Deborahs out there? More Sandras?

I looked him over again, his whole body slouched back into the cheap plastic seat. This act, this nonchalance, might fool the rest of the world but it didn't fool me. I knew what lay behind it.

Things aren't going quite according to plan, are they Gary? I spoke to him in my mind. *It's not working. It's time to quit.*

I felt my strength returning. I wasn't going to let this freak beat me.

If he wanted a partner in crime, I'd give him one. I'd show him exactly what he wanted to see. And then, well, we'd see...

Chapter Seventeen
The Outside

'Hey, let's get you some clothes today,' Gary said the next morning as he made coffee. He'd poured me a large bowl of Cheerios that I was mechanically shoveling into my mouth. I hardly tasted food any more. It was just fuel to get me from one day to the next.

Usually I loved shopping – there was nothing I enjoyed more than spending hours among the rails of clothes at the mall, wandering leisurely from one store to the next, picking up this, trying on that, seeing what new fashion suited me.

But the thought of shopping with Gary did not fill me with excitement. I wasn't going to let him know that, however.

'Yeah – this is definitely not my favorite outfit,' I scoffed, indicating the baggy jumper and jeans, the legs pooling around my feet. 'I could do with some underwear for a start!'

I wasn't Gary's slave anymore, I was his partner – that's what he thought – so I talked to him like a partner.

There was no fawning gratitude, no slavish devotion. The whole reason I was up here to begin with was because he thought I was part of his sick enterprise so I wasn't going to act like his offering to get me clothes was some great gesture of generosity.

'Okay,' he agreed. 'Just give me a few minutes and we'll go to the store.'

I picked up a cup of coffee and walked back into the living room to finish my breakfast. He took a couple of sandwiches down to the girls and was back up in a few minutes.

In some strange way I could see he was enjoying this. This was what he wanted all along, someone he could share his life with, and now he had it. He had me. Even if there was some small doubt in his mind about the way things were going, he wasn't going to let it bother him. He wanted us to be together.

We got in the car and drove to a thrift store round the corner where the signs above the racks boasted pathetically low prices. And the clothes matched the signs.

Gary might have been driving around in a Rolls and a Cadillac but he sure as hell didn't spend any more money then was strictly necessary. All the food on his kitchen counter was supermarket own brands – the cheap stuff. Apart from the fringed brown leather jacket, his clothes were cheap and nasty. And here we were browsing the rejected rails of other people's wardrobes.

We walked in together and I stopped for a minute to get my bearings – I was focused completely on the task, not looking around, not thinking about escape.

I still didn't know how it was going to happen, I was working everything out minute to minute, but I knew now was not the time. He had to trust me completely, he had to believe that I wasn't going to betray him, that's what my instincts told me, and we weren't there yet. Not yet.

So I found the aisle with the knickers first and grabbed a couple of pairs in my size. Then I located the jeans and pulled out a couple of pairs of size 6s. Gary was at my side the whole time and I was careful to act like he was my boyfriend accompanying me on an ordinary shopping trip. Not too fast, not too slow. Casual, like we'd done this all before.

I slung the jeans in his direction and he held them dutifully, following me to the next rail, where I picked out a couple of T-shirts and put those in his arms too.

Finally, I found a brown jacket and a blue polo-necked jumper.

'That'll do,' I told him.

He nodded and we headed over to the counter.

I didn't bother getting any bras – I was small enough not to have to worry about those and frankly I was exhausted now with the concentration and the energy. I just wanted to get out of there.

He couldn't tell but I was on tenterhooks the whole time. I knew that just one look in the wrong direction, one misplaced word and I could be back down in that basement again. I turned my back to the cashier at the till as she rang up the items, leaning, arms crossed against the counter as if I couldn't care less.

In truth, I just didn't want her to talk to me or look at me. It could be dangerous.

He paid with a $20 bill and we left with our purchases in two plastic carrier bags. I'd never endured such a miserable shopping trip in my life.

When we got back I disappeared upstairs to put on the new clothes. Everything fit fine and it was a relief to be out of the strange baggy pants and oversized man's shirt.

Now I went into the bathroom and looked in the small circular face mirror over the sink – I'd already tried to tame my hair by pulling it back into a tight ponytail and tying it with an elastic band I'd found in the living room.

Now I splashed water over my face and smoothed down my hair.

I stood there for a moment, saying my name in my head: *Josefina Rivera.*

Josefina Rivera. You will survive this, Josefina. You are strong. You are a fighter. You adapt.

Then I let out a long sigh, pushed back my shoulders and marched downstairs.

Gary looked up from the sofa in the living room where he was watching TV.

'That's better,' he said, admiringly. 'You're sure shaping up a lot better now.'

'I should think so,' I retorted. 'At least I can see my waist again!'

I was flexing my powers now, adding a little tartness to my voice, a slight disdain. *Let him feel lucky to have me here at all*, I thought. *I don't want this guy even considering chaining me up again.*

* * *

Later I was making coffee in the kitchen. Every time I went in there now I averted my eyes from the cooker where the pot still stood with Sandra's head in it.

I concentrated on what I was doing, I didn't open the freezer. I didn't look in the fridge. I didn't want to see those grisly sights again.

Gary came in.

'I need to take the Rolls to the shop,' he said. 'You can follow me in the Caddy so we got a way of getting back afterwards.'

'Sure,' I said.

There was a pause.

Then: 'You a good driver?'

I almost choked on my coffee.

He was concerned about his precious car! *Sure, kill two women but look after your wheels!* This guy had it all back to front.

'I'm an excellent driver,' I told him confidently. It was one more step in the right direction. He trusted me enough to hand me the keys to the car, he must have believed that I wasn't just going to drive it straight to the first cop shop I came across. And he was right. Where would that have got me? If he knew I wasn't following him he could get back to the house, kill the girls and go on the run. And then what would I be left with? A lifetime of looking over my shoulder, wondering when he was going to pop up next, knowing that my life was only as long as the distance between us.

We went into the garage and he handed me the keys to the Cadillac. I slid into the driver's side and the first thing I had to do was adjust the seat. He was a lot taller than me and the way he had it, I couldn't even reach the pedals.

He got into the Rolls and pulled slowly out of the drive. I put the car into gear and let the powerful engine inch me steadily forward. It was a beautiful car. The engine hummed smoothly beneath me. I tried not to let myself think of all the other times I'd driven. All those other occasions when I'd been free to go where I wanted, whenever I liked. Now I was in the driving seat but I wasn't in control. Gary pulled out onto the street and I rolled out behind him, careful to keep a small distance between us.

I saw him checking his rear-view mirror, his eyes flicking upwards to check I was still there. *Don't worry, Gary.* I was thinking. *I'm not going anywhere. Not yet.*

We turned a few corners, and a few heads, as we rode through the slum area of Philadelphia, a Rolls-Royce followed by a Cadillac, both in immaculate condition. They were not everyday sights around here, I was sure of that.

But I was holding my nerve, not daring to make eye contact with the streetwalkers and moms pushing prams on the sidewalk.

In a few minutes we turned into the car shop. Gary rolled his window down with his arm resting on the side of the car.

He shouted out to the mechanic tinkering under the bonnet of a Chevy, 'Hey, Mike!'

Mike appeared from behind the hood wearing a pair of grubby blue overalls and wiping a wrench with a blackened cloth.

'Hey, Gary!' Mike seemed like a normal person who knew Gary in the real world, the world which Gary checked in and out of like a hotel guest. Mike could clearly see me behind Gary in his Cadillac. I guess he recognized Gary's cars.

'The Rolls is hers too!' Gary shouted genially, thumbing back at me.

'Lucky girl!' Mike shot back. *Yeah*, I was thinking – *lucky, lucky me*.

Gary now exited the Rolls-Royce and went over to speak to Mike. They had a conversation, too far away for me to overhear. I took the time to get out of the driver's seat and move into the passenger seat. Gary may have thought I was his partner now but I knew he wasn't ready for me to be in the driver's seat. And I wasn't going to push my luck.

A short while later Gary got back in the car and pulled out of the car shop. I wondered whether the Rolls needed work at all or whether Gary was setting up an alibi.

He wanted other people to see me with him, he wanted them to believe I was his girlfriend, that I was there of my own free will. If ever the cops came round his way, my presence would deflect any potential suspicion away from him.

All these girls have gone missing but it couldn't be him, right? He had a girlfriend. Me.

* * *

Gary went to bed early and got up late.

I was constantly aware of the women still chained up below our feet but Gary carried on as if they weren't there. Whenever he went down to give them food or have sex, I stayed upstairs. What were they thinking, I wondered?

What did they think I was doing up here?

Every day now I was getting stronger, more confident. Gary didn't try and have sex with me at night. He still thought I was pregnant. And I did too. In the whole time I'd been here I'd not had a period. I tried not to let myself think of the baby growing inside me. It wasn't something I wanted. I knew it would never live. There was no way I could keep a baby born out of this hideous situation.

I spent the majority of my time in the living room and kitchen, taking showers every morning to try and rid my body of the stink of Gary's musty bed sheets.

Then, six days after I was freed of the chains, I heard it. I heard my opening.

That day he told me: 'I want to get another girl.'

Chapter Eighteen
Poker

There is a point in every poker game when you have to decide whether to bluff. You may be losing big time, or it may be that you expected to get a big hand on a promising start but you don't – the cards just aren't on your side. But you need a win and if you don't have the cards, and it looks like nobody else does either, then you have a choice: fold or bluff.

I was always a good poker player. As a teenager I'd learned the basic rules of the game but the skill, the art of playing poker, came naturally. You can't teach someone how to bluff or when to judge the right time to go all-in.

It's more than just a game, it's a lesson in observation. Can you tell what the others in the game have got by the way they are betting? Do their facial expressions, or small tics, give anything away? It's not just about having the cards, you have to be an expert in reading people.

And you have to be an expert in fooling them too.

I used to play a lot of poker with my friends and I rarely lost big money. I had a good sense of when to bet big and how to bluff my way to a snagging a large pot.

At the point where you can see the other players thinking about it, at the very moment when they are deciding whether to fold or bluff, then you go all-in.

That is the moment, the moment you know you could lose it all. But the moment at which you have to raise the stakes. Sky high. You make it too dangerous for your competitors to play on.

You make them think there's no way this girl has got anything less than a brilliant hand. But there is only one way they're going to find that out, and that is to make them pay to see you.

And that looks far too expensive. So they fold.

* * *

Until this moment I had no idea how I was going to try to escape. I was taking each day as it came, hour-by-hour, minute-by-minute.

I prayed to God for guidance and then, when it happened, when my chance came, I didn't hesitate. I went all-in.

'Okay,' I said. 'I'll go with you to get a girl. And then after that I want to see my family. I can't take you with me because, you know, there's going to be a whole lot of questions since I've been gone a long time and they're going to be very upset. Give me a chance to talk to them and explain to them what is going on, that I've got an old man and we were away. Smooth things over. And then I'll come back and get you and you can meet everybody.'

'Okay, fine.'

And that was it. I didn't need to say anymore. He agreed. Although I knew all about Gary and his background, the fact was he still didn't know an awful lot about me. All he knew was that I had kids – I hadn't revealed to him that they weren't living with me or who exactly I meant when I said 'my family'.

But I didn't need to give him any more details – he said yes and that was all I needed.

Since then I've frequently wondered why he agreed so readily. Did he want to be caught? Was he ready for it all to be over? I don't know. In some way I think he was just so convinced that we were in this together, it didn't occur to him that I wouldn't do as I said.

He had what he wanted: somebody who cared about him, somebody who knew and understood his plight.

If it had been me, I would never have agreed. I would have looked straight at me and said, 'What? Do you think I'm stupid?'

Whether he trusted me or just wanted the whole thing to end, I for one was definitely ready for it to be done and over with. I'd been captured in November, it was now the end of March. Yes, I was ready for it all to end.

It was around 7 p.m. when we headed out in the Cadillac. It was a cool, breezy night and we were cruising slowly down Front Street when we saw a girl I recognized standing on the street corner. I knew her as Vickie from a time when we both worked at a strip club called Hearts and Flowers but I later came to learn her name was Agnes Adams.

'Hey Gary! Gary!' she was calling out and waving from across the street. Clearly she knew Gary too.

Gary stopped the car and she got in the back seat. She noticed me next to Gary: 'Oh Nicole! How you doing?'

I managed a faint: 'Hey Vickie.' And Gary and Vickie had a quick conversation. They'd been together before and he was offering her the same deal as last time: $30 to go back to his, which she readily agreed to.

This ain't good, I was thinking. *This ain't good at all.*

But in my mind I was trying not to focus on Vickie – I was playing the long game and if things went right and my massive gamble paid off, she wouldn't be in the basement too long.

For now, I was just trying to keep cool, trying to keep up the act that had so far convinced Gary that I was on his side. We'd made a deal. I helped him get a girl, he let me go see my family. As long as that held up then she should come out of this okay.

But the stakes couldn't have been higher. I knew that one wrong move, one wrong word at any time, and it could all go wrong. This wasn't a game I could afford to lose. For my sake or any of the others.

Gary drove us both back to North Marshall Street and I stayed downstairs in the living room while he took Vickie up to the bedroom. It was only about fifteen minutes later when he brought her down naked in the cuffs.

Maybe it was the fact that I was there and acting really casual that put her at her ease, maybe it was the fact that she knew Gary from before, but Vickie was very nonchalant as he marched her down the steps to the basement.

She didn't cry and she didn't seem mad either. Gary shot a look at me and jerked his head in the direction of the basement, a silent command: *Follow me.*

So for the first time since I was freed I followed him down to the basement. The other girls looked up as we came down – it was a strange, uneasy meeting. They stared at me, wide-eyed with confusion and mistrust.

I was instantly on edge back down there in that basement: the familiar dank smell, the bright light and bare walls. Claustrophobia clawed at my skin, making it hard to think and breathe normally.

Meanwhile Gary was going through the routine with the muffler clamps and Vickie was calm as you like, just sort of standing there, nodding to the other girls.

This one is clueless, I thought.

'Get in the hole,' he instructed and, nice as pie, she got in and sat down. Gary replaced the board on top.

The other girls were looking straight at me but I couldn't meet their gaze – I couldn't face them. I knew what they were thinking: *She's gone over to his side. Now we're all doomed.*

I desperately wanted to grab them and tell them – *it's okay, we're nearly free. Just trust me. Hang in there.* But of course I couldn't say a word. I couldn't let my poker face slip for an instant.

We were on the cusp of freedom but nobody knew it except me.

This had to work. It just had to. Failure wasn't an option.

By the time Gary and I got back upstairs it was nearly nine. 'Okay,' Gary said. 'Let's do your thing now.'

He seemed satisfied that I'd fulfilled my part of the bargain so we got in the Cadillac again and drove up to Six and Gerard, near where Gary picked me up.

I indicated a gas station at the corner.

'Pull in here,' I told him. 'You can wait here while I go and talk to them. Grab a cup of coffee and I'll be back in twenty minutes or so.'

My heart was pounding so hard, I was surprised he couldn't hear it. He seemed content with the whole set-up – in his mind I was now his partner, I was going to find a way to convince my family everything was okay and then he'd keep right on going with his crazy plans.

I got out the car and walked slowly down the street – I couldn't be seen to rush this, he mustn't get an inkling of what I had planned. If he did, it could all fall apart in an instant.

So I headed down Gerard Street and after one block I turned a corner where I knew there was a phone box. I was striding now, long purposeful steps, and almost fell into the phone box like a drowning man reaching for a rescue raft.

My hands shook as I lifted the receiver and dialed 911 – I knew what I was going to say, I'd been rehearsing this for weeks. As soon as I was put through to the police I started speaking, fast but clear: 'Listen, I don't have a whole lot of time. I've been kidnapped and held for four months in this guy's basement. I've been shackled, beaten and tortured. There are other girls still there. The guy that did it is waiting for me at the gas station at Six and Gerard. I need somebody to come out here and pick him up so that he can't get back to these other girls because if he does he's going to kill them.'

There was a pause on the end of the line.

'Erm, can you tell us that again, Miss?'

Oh Jesus! I knew that while I was here every second counted. How long had I been gone now? Three minutes, maybe more?

They didn't believe me – they didn't even understand me so I explained my story again and this time I added: 'Can you please just send someone out now. I'm at the phone booth at 5th and Gerard. Please! This is a matter of life and death.'

The voice on the other end of the phone still sounded skeptical but he said, 'Okay, what do you have on?'

I described my outfit and he said, 'Stay right there on that corner. We're sending a car out now.'

'Okay.' I put the phone down. My hands were still trembling and I grasped them together under my chin. Now I stepped outside the phone box and stood there on the corner, my eyes darting up and down the road, looking out for the police car, and also the Cadillac. It could be either.

The seconds ticked by so slowly, I felt like screaming. *Come on, come on, come on!* I stomped my feet on the floor, hopping from one foot to the other – to keep warm or to stop myself going insane, I wasn't sure which.

Just then I saw a man I recognized turn the corner, with a few of his friends. His name was Vincent Nelson – we used to live on the same apartment block. We used to get high together – but that wasn't unusual, in this part of the world everyone got high together. He spotted me immediately.

'Nicole! What's up?' He seemed happy to see me and judging by his movements and the way he was walking I reckoned he must be high right now. It was funny, in the whole time I'd been captive I hadn't once thought of taking drugs.

'Where have you been?' he drawled. 'We ain't seen you for months.'

'I can't talk now, Vincent. I'll tell you later,' I muttered irritably, trying to get rid of him.

'Shit, Nicole! You disappear for months and we just want to know what's up!'

'Look,' I was losing my rag now. 'I got kidnapped, okay? I got caught up in some mess and we'll talk about it some other time. Please, just leave it.'

Vincent shrugged and by now his friends were dragging him off down the street. 'I'll catch you later!' he shouted as he wandered off.

The minutes dragged by so slowly. My heart was racing. I was jittery, breathing hard. Were they ever going to get here? Would I have to call them back?

Finally, after ten minutes, a police paddy wagon turned the corner and pulled up next to me.

Two cops got out the car.

'Okay, Miss. We got some very strange call from you so can you tell us again what's going on?'

Christ!

'Look, I'm gonna explain this to you one more time,' I said, panic starting to rise in my voice. 'Because all this... this talking! This is detrimental. There are other girls there. This guy Gary Heidnik has kidnapped me and he's had me chained and shackled in his basement for four months. Me and some other girls – he's killed two already. And we've all been raped, tortured and beaten. Look!'

I hoiked up the bottom of my jeans to show him the back of my legs where the shackle marks were still red and sore.

That convinced them.

'Okay,' he said. 'You stay here. We're gonna go back there and pick him up and we'll have another car come here and meet you.'

He got back in the wagon while his partner radioed the station to get another car to meet me. When it pulled up, they took off.

This time a black lady cop got out of the car.

'Unbelievable!' she complained loudly as she heaved her bulky frame out of the driver's seat. 'I'm getting ready to get off work and now I have to come down here and sit with *you*?'

She was so mad, it was almost laughable.

We were there a couple of minutes before her radio went off.

'Get in.' She motioned for me to get in the back. 'I got to take you to the gas station. They want to make sure they got the right guy.'

I nodded. I was ready for this. So I got in the back of the car and we drove the short distance to the gas station. When we got there I could see Gary's Cadillac still parked at the side but he wasn't in it. Oh no! Did they lose him? Did he run?

I was gripped with panic and fear.

But then I looked over to the paddy wagon and the cops opened up the car door and there he was, sitting there with his hands cuffed behind him. I almost smiled with relief.

'Yup, that's him,' I said. Gary looked directly at me but didn't say a word. I could tell what he was thinking – *I know I shouldn't have trusted you.*

I breathed out for what felt like the first time that night. Relief washed over me. It was over. It was finally over. I'd won.

The lady cop drove me over to the Sex Crimes Unit in the police station where a specialist from the unit took care of me, a lovely lady called Mary, someone that didn't treat me like a nuisance or a waste of her time. Mary offered me a cheese sandwich and a soda then led me through to an interview room where a female detective was sitting at a desk.

'We need you to go through everything in detail,' she explained. 'We need to know where everything is because we don't want to make any mistakes. We're gonna get a warrant so we can go into every part of the house that we need to. So it's very important you tell us everything. Right from the start.'

So I started talking and once I started, I couldn't stop. It all came pouring out of me. I told them everything that had happened to me in the last four months, everything I'd seen, heard and experienced. I told them about Sandra, about how he cut her up into little bits and boiled her head on the stove and roasted her ribs in the oven. I told them about the dog food and how he fed bits of her to the other girls. I tell them about the electrocution, about Deborah Dudley dying, about the letter Gary made me sign, and how it earned me my freedom. I told them about dumping her body in the Pine Barrens and about the three girls still there in his basement, alive. I described the house in perfect detail, telling them where the girls were being kept. But as I spoke I could see the shock on their faces. This was unbelievable, they were thinking. And as I listened to myself talking, I realized I was thinking the same. It was unbelievable to me too. I'd lived it and I found it too crazy, too beyond comprehension to fully take it all in.

By the time I'd finished it was the early hours of the morning and the police got the search warrant they needed to send their team into the house.

They reported back to me an hour later.

'The house was so normal we couldn't believe that anything was going on there but it was just like you said. The girls didn't even make any noise when we came in – they thought it was Heidnik playing a trick. We had to get bolt cutters to free them from the shackles. We've taken them to the hospital to get checked over and that's where we're gonna take you now.'

I was driven to the hospital just as the sun came up on a new day, my first day of freedom. I hadn't slept, I'd barely eaten but I wasn't tired or hungry.

In the hospital they conducted a full examination and took blood samples. I was sat in the lobby waiting for the results when I saw Vickie coming out of one of the rooms.

'That's her,' she shrieked, pointing at me. 'That's the one who kidnapped me! I told you it was a girl and there she is!'

I just sat there and shook my head.

After a few minutes I was called back into the doctor's office.

'Well, you're lucky,' he said. 'You're not pregnant.'

Thank God for that! I wanted to smile but I didn't quite understand.

'But I didn't get a period for four months,' I said.

'Well, it was probably the stress of the situation,' the doctor explained. 'That, combined with the fact that you were eating very little. Don't worry, it'll come.'

Just a few hours later my period arrived. I was hugely relieved that I didn't have to go through the emotional turmoil of an abortion. But also, I felt triumphant.

It didn't work. None of his plans had worked.

Even my body found a way to beat you, Gary Heidnik!

Chapter Nineteen
Freedom

'You think you can remember where he left the body?' a cop asked me. We were back at the police station. I'd still not had a shower or slept but I was so wired I couldn't even think of sleeping.

'I'll do the best that I can,' I told him. I'd thought about this, I knew they'd want to recover the body and I'd attempted to make a mental map when Gary took me there so I was prepared for this moment.

The station was now a hive of activity – cops ran backwards and forwards, carrying bags and bags of stuff. I learned later it was all the evidence recovered from Heidnik's house – those coppers didn't take any chances. They took out everything and they made a list so long it took them eleven days to compile.

Now I was sitting in an interview room nursing a strong cup of coffee and the officer in charge of the case came to get me.

'Okay, let's go,' he said.

We got into the car park and that's when the enormity of what was going on hit me.

There was press everywhere! We could hardly hear for

the whumping of the news choppers overhead. The parking lot was full of reporters and every type of news vehicle you could imagine.

The moment I stepped outside the shouts started up and a million cameras flashed in my face. I was temporarily blinded.

'Nicole! Nicole!' they hollered at me. Microphones were shoved towards me; even the detectives appeared overwhelmed.

The press was everywhere and they were all clamoring to speak to me. I didn't say a word, it was too much for me to take in. The two detectives immediately swung into action, one making a path through the crowd, shouting, 'Let us through! Out the way!' while the other shielded me with his large body, protecting me from the hands and voices and faces and questions that came at me from every angle.

It seemed to take ages but we slowly pushed our way through the crowds and I let the officers bundle me into the back of the car. Once we were inside, me in the back with the two detectives up front, we all sat back in stunned silence. I never even expected one reporter to be there, let alone thousands. I just never considered the media in this at all.

I listened to the helicopters circling above us.

The detectives started up the car but we were surrounded. It took us forever to move through the swarm of cars and people.

'This is just ridiculous!' the detective who was driving exclaimed.

We all looked up now at the choppers – one, two, three. *How many of those damn things have they got up there?* I wondered.

I noticed the sides of each were marked with the logo of TV channels – Channel 6, Channel 3, CNN, CBS.

We edged out onto the road and now we were travelling in a massive convoy – dozens of cars trailing behind us, the choppers following too.

'Why are all these press here?' I asked, dazed.

The officer answered me: 'You don't even realize how big this story is, do you?'

'No.'

'Well, this will probably be an ongoing thing. Try not to pay them any mind.'

I don't know how you can ignore a succession of eager, clamoring press – they followed us all the way across the bridge. There was a huge cavalcade of vehicles: press cars, more police cars, helicopters.

I just hoped I could remember where Gary dumped Deborah's body. We headed out now towards New Jersey – the Pine Barrens is a million acres. It covers a quarter of the state. I knew the chances of finding her in all that forest were practically nil but still, I was going to do my best.

Now we were travelling down the same road I went along with Gary just a few days before and the signs were familiar. But once we were out in the Barrens, there were no landmarks, nothing to indicate where we'd stopped.

Still, my senses were in a heightened state of alert. I didn't want to get this wrong. I'm usually terrible with directions! But I was so upset at the thought of Deborah just lying out in the forest, dumped like a pile of rubbish, I was determined to try my best.

The miles drifted past us, the noise overhead still deafening. Suddenly, I felt we were nearing the spot. I told the cops to slow down.

'Okay, okay,' I said, biting my nails anxiously, scanning the rows of trees. This felt close. 'Here! It's here!'

We turned off into what looked like the same clearing I stopped at with Gary.

I directed them to keep going a little way then we came to a stop.

Behind, the other cop car had screeched up behind us and two cops got out, ordering the media pack to keep back.

I pointed over in the direction Heidnik had walked. 'He took her over there. Not far, maybe ten, twenty steps.'

I was just guessing – after all, it was dark when we came here with Deborah.

'You wait here,' the cop ordered and they got out.

They set off on foot in the direction I'd given them and the next thing I heard was: 'Whoa! Whoa! We got her! We got her!'

I sent up a silent prayer: *Rest in peace, Deborah. Now you can rest in peace.*

Another cop car pulled up behind us and two more cops went over to the body – I didn't get out, I didn't want to see. A few minutes later an ambulance pulled up and the detectives returned to the car.

'I'd like to see my family now, please,' I told them.

* * *

On the way back the detective radioed the station and they told him to take me to the office of the Assistant District Attorney, a man called Charles Gallagher.

Gallagher was the man in charge – he greeted me solemnly but with genuine warmth.

'I'm going to try to do everything I can to make you comfortable,' he said, his eyes full of concern. 'We got your kids coming to see you and we've arranged for you to stay in a hotel for now. It's a secret location so the press can't get to you. The fact is, we don't know at this stage if Heidnik had any accomplices so we're going to give you as much protection as you need.'

'Thank you,' I said. Everything was happening so fast. 'What about my apartment?'

'That's gone.' He shook his head. 'When you didn't show up for a few weeks, the landlord got rid of your stuff and rented it out again. It's not yours anymore.'

'Oh.' A part of me felt very sad at this news. It was meant to be a new start for me, that apartment. A new life. Now it was gone and it dawned on me that I *was* starting a new life now, but one very different from that I'd imagined for myself.

Suddenly I was consumed with fury at Heidnik – he'd

changed everything. I'd had a plan. I wanted to get my life on track. He'd taken that from me. But there was no time to think about this.

'You want to speak to your mom?' Gallagher asked gently. 'She's eager to hear your voice.'

I almost cried with happiness. My mom! So much time had passed and for so long I'd wondered if I'd ever see her again. I nodded, holding my hand to my mouth to stifle a small sob.

Gallagher led me into his office – he was a small, intent-looking man, only around forty, but inside you could tell he was driven, he was someone with strong and deep convictions.

He sat me down at his desk and minutes later they'd patched my mom through on his line.

'Josie?' Just hearing her voice made me weep.

For a few seconds I couldn't speak.

Then: 'Mom. It's me – I'm okay.'

'Well, this is some mess you've got yourself into!'

I couldn't help but laugh. 'You're telling me!'

'We didn't know what had happened to you. You missed Thanksgiving and then Christmas and LaToya's birthday. I knew you wouldn't have missed her birthday so I went to the apartment looking for you and nobody said they'd seen you. I went to your friends. I said to them, "You don't have to tell me where she is but just let me know if she's okay." They said, "Honestly, Mrs Patterson. We're real worried. We ain't seen her either." So that's when I reported you to the police. But nobody had any idea where you were.

'I only knew they'd found you when I saw the reports on the news. I was in the kitchen washing up and there's this helicopter following a police car and the news reporter is saying: "Josefina Rivera is leading the cops to the victim's body."

'That's when they cut to a picture of you sat in the back of the police car and I nearly drop the dishes I'm drying! Oh baby! I'm so pleased you're okay!'

'Can you come and see me, Mom?' I asked in a small voice. I just needed to see her and hold her again.

'I'm coming, honey. Don't you worry, Momma's coming.'

* * *

The next few hours passed by in a blur – someone brought me toast. I talked to Mary, who worked for Victims' Compensation, and she took me out to buy clothes. When we returned to the DS's office, Charles Gallagher was smiling at me.

'We got your family coming,' he said.

I was so excited, I could hardly sit still. I paced back and forth in the office. Then the door opened and Billy came in, Toya trailing behind him.

Her face lit up when she saw me and she ran into my arms.

'Oh Bookie, Bookie!' I said, using my pet name for her, and breathed into her neck, squeezing her hard and letting the tears fall freely.

She just went right on hugging me, unwilling to let me go.

Eventually I unhooked her little fingers from round my neck and took her by the hand to sit next to me on the couch.

'Are you okay, Bookie?'

She nodded. 'Mmm. I'm fine. I had some strange dreams, Mom. I dreamt you were in a hole somewhere surrounded by money. And you couldn't get out.'

I stared at her in disbelief. How could she know that? Nobody knew that.

But I didn't tell her anything – she was just a child. She didn't need to know what had happened to me.

'Well, Mommy's back now and she's fine. I'm so sorry I missed your birthday honey. Are you okay? You doing okay in school? Are you being a good girl for your daddy?'

I drilled her, all the while stroking her hair and trying to keep the tears at bay.

Next, a Hispanic couple I'd not seen before came in. They were accompanied by a woman who identified herself as Ricky and Zornae's social worker.

'These people here are the little ones' foster parents – Mr and Mrs Sepulveda,' she said. 'They're gonna bring the kids in to see you.'

I nodded, mutely. It was all so much to take in.

The wife disappeared into the lobby again and when she returned she was holding a chubby baby in one arm and a small, scared-looking girl toddled next to her.

'Oh my babies!' I exclaimed. The lady handed me the baby – it was Ricky, although I hardly recognized him now. The last time I'd seen him he was just a few weeks old, an infant, now he was a proper little baby. Five months old.

Before, he was light caramel and now he was a deep rich brown, a whole different color! I was shocked. The last time I'd seen him I'd changed his clothes, stroked his head and whispered to him about how I was going to make a great life for us. We were mother and son, bonded.

I wanted to feel that love again, that connection, but I couldn't. Too much had happened and I wasn't the same woman.

And he didn't seem like my baby anymore.

All I wanted to say was 'Are you sure this is my baby?' as I cradled him.

Zornae, dressed in a blue and white spotty playsuit, huddled behind the Hispanic lady she'd clearly got used to calling Mom, too scared to come out and greet me.

'Go say hi to your momma!' the lady instructed her. 'That's your mom.'

But the girl just retreated even further behind the lady's legs. Now she was completely enveloped in her skirts and I was struck with sadness.

She didn't recognize me. She didn't even know who I was. This baby, who I'd loved and nurtured and cared for, who'd shared a bed with Toya and amused us for hours with her giggling and gurgling, was a stranger to me now.

It was a blow to my heart. My anger towards Heidnik returned – *he's done this to me. He's taken my children away.*

I hated it. Hated it. But I understood why Zornae reacted like this – I remembered the same feeling I'd had when my dad came to see me as a child.

'Come on now, little one,' the lady bent down to Zornae, switching into fluent Spanish that I didn't understand, urging her towards me. I tried to catch a little of what she was saying but with my schoolgirl Spanish, I felt cut out of their exchange.

The little girl put her arms out to the lady and she lifted her up – she was clearly besotted with the little girl and I felt like an outsider looking in on a happy family scene.

My family, these children were my family and yet they were reaching for the arms of a stranger.

'It's okay,' I said. 'Don't worry. Don't pressure her.'

Why should these children suffer anymore? I had already brought them enough pain and confusion – they didn't need any more pressure in their lives. I ached with guilt and remorse.

I turned my attention back to LaToya and we started to play a game she had brought along. Ten minutes later my mom opened the door.

I raced into her arms and she whispered in my ear, 'I love you, honey.'

Suddenly I could give way to all the confused feelings of the past hour and let my mom hold me.

I wept like a child and we stood there in an embrace for a while before my mom pulled back to give me a quick appraisal.

'You look fine, just fine,' she said as I wiped away the tears, whether to reassure her or myself I couldn't tell.

'I'm doing okay, Mom,' I said, though I wasn't really sure if that was true.

I wanted to tell her everything – all about the pain, the torture, the rapes and the deaths. But I didn't – with the kids there it wouldn't have been right to go into any details of what happened.

We played with the kids for a while and Mom told me all about the news I'd missed out on.

Then she asked, 'You got somewhere to go?'

'They're putting us in hotels,' I said.

She nodded with approval. 'You get yourself some sleep now, you hear? You look like you could do with some good rest.'

I smiled, gratefully. An hour later, the cops returned to say they'd got the welfare lady in to see me. I said a hurried goodbye to everyone and then I was back in the hands of the police.

I barely had time to think about what had just happened with the kids – it was confusing and upsetting but I put it to the back of my mind. *No time now*, I told myself. *Just keep yourself together Josefina. You're free. There'll be time to come.*

Mary had already notified welfare that I'd been kidnapped for the past four months so now they had to reinstate my claim. But I couldn't go to the office so they sent someone round to the DA's office to reopen my file.

It was a small administrative task to get me a photo ID made up in order to get all my welfare back payments but important. At that stage I had no money at all, not one cent or possession to my name.

In the early evening I was taken out the back door to where a police car was waiting to take me to a nearby hotel

– every time I stepped outside it was astonishing to me. Just feeling the breeze on my face, seeing the setting sun light up an otherwise dull day with a warm amber glow. It was glorious. I was free! But not quite free enough. The police couldn't risk letting me out the front where hundreds of reporters still gathered, waiting impatiently for the next development in the story. The police car wasted no time – we took off like a bullet, zooming through the busy rush hour streets, lights blazing, just in case we were being followed, until we came to a small hotel on the edge of town.

We walked up a couple of flights and they let me into a large suite. I begged for some moments alone and the cops waited outside my room. I yearned for this, space and silence.

I was alone for the first time in months. I was here, out, alive.

For the first time since my escape, I took a shower. The warm water bounced off my skin. A million images swam through my mind – the Pine Barrens, Deborah's body, my kids moving away from me, Mom's face, concerned, but trying to hide it, the police, Gallagher, the helicopters…

I stepped outside the shower and toweled myself down. I inspected my body – I still wore the scars of the chains on my ankles.

Where is Heidnik now? I wondered. *I hope that bastard is in chains.*

I dressed in the clothes I'd bought earlier with Mary.

The cops knocked an hour later. 'We've got your sister here to see you. She insisted on coming.'

He'd hardly finished speaking when Iris barged her way past and we hugged each other.

'Jesus girl!' she said. 'Are you okay? We all been so worried about you. Do you know what they're saying? They're saying you were beaten and tortured and made to eat other people and shit like that. Man, that's so fucked up!'

'It wasn't me. I didn't have to eat it,' I said. 'He made the other girls. But yeah, all that other stuff is true. It's too much, Iris. Too much.'

'Look, you're safe now. You'll be okay.'

I was relieved that she was there with me now, I felt stronger, safer in her presence.

In truth, it made me feel a little bit normal – she was a physical reminder of my past and of who I was, or at least, who I used to be.

At this moment I wasn't sure how much of my past remained.

'Stay the night with me?' I asked. 'I don't want to be alone tonight.'

'Sure,' she agreed.

We sat on the bed in the room and I told her what had happened to me. At some point, we got room service delivered – burger and fries each – while the police came in and out to ask me questions.

A detective was more or less permanently at my side, getting instructions from the station, taking notes.

At 10 p.m. I switched on the TV to catch the news – I needed to know what they were saying about all of this.

'… and now we can go to the hotel where we're talking to one of the victims,' the news anchor handed smoothly over to the reporter on the ground who I could clearly see was standing outside the ground floor of our very hotel.

'What the fuck!' I exclaimed. Now the detective next to me was also staring at the screen, his face contorted in anger.

Agnes Adams – Vickie – stood at the window of her bedroom in the hotel, chatting away to the reporter outside.

'How are they talking to her?' I demanded. 'I thought this was supposed to be a secret location!'

'Yeah, it was!' he said through gritted teeth. 'What in the hell does she think she's doing?'

The camera panned around – you could clearly see there were dozens of other reporters crammed outside Agnes's window.

The detective got up off the bed and shifted my curtain aside a little way, just to get a look outside.

'Shit!' he said. 'They're down there. Listen, don't worry, we won't let any of them in. You're on the third floor so you'll be fine. Just stay here for tonight. We'll have to move you in the morning.'

If it wasn't for Iris I don't think I would have fallen asleep that night. Everything had happened so fast – the sheer volume and interest from the press was overwhelming. That first night they tracked us down. And they would do so time and time again in the many long, difficult months to come.

At least I escaped from Heidnik after four months – with the press, it went on for years.

Chapter Twenty
A New Reality

I came to in darkness.

Darkness and the faint buzzing of an air conditioner in the background. Where was I? I looked about me – an anonymous hotel room, a woman asleep in the twin bed next to mine, bland furnishings, crisp white sheets, the smell of air freshener and frying bacon from somewhere.

Was this real? Was I still chained in Heidnik's basement on North Marshall Street, asleep and dreaming this strange place? I was certain that at any moment now I'd wake up with chains around my ankles.

My head returned to the pillow and I shut my eyes again. But the next time I woke up, I was in the same place, only now the sunlight streamed through the paper-thin curtains. Iris was already up, making an instant coffee from the tiny kettle in the corner of the room.

Reality had been turned upside down. I didn't know where I was or what I was doing here. I let myself lie there for a while as it all slowly came back to me – escaping, the police station, finding Deborah, my family.

The relief lasted only a few minutes as someone knocked loudly at the door. A confident, loud and insistent: Bang bang bang!

The door shuddered with the impact. Iris looked back at me and I nodded: yes, I'm awake.

She went to answer it. I heard the voice of the police officer faintly from the bed. 'We'll need to move her soon. Can you make sure she gets up and eats breakfast? We've only got half an hour.'

I dragged my weary body to the bathroom – suddenly all the adrenaline of the past twenty-four hours had left me. Every part of me ached, I just wanted to go back to bed and sleep for a week, but I couldn't.

* * *

I was free now but not in a way I could recognize. I was surrounded by people the whole time and my movements were restricted to the places the police wanted me to be.

I was taken to the DA's office for more admin, more questions, and then back to the station to give more statements. In the meantime I was moved to a different hotel. Now all the girls were being kept apart, just in case the media uncovered one of us. And there were gagging orders on us so we weren't allowed to speak to the media.

I was driven to a women's mental health unit for psychological assessment. I saw two psychiatrists, who both wanted to admit me.

But I'd had enough and insisted on speaking to Gallagher on the phone. I felt edgy, upset and impatient.

'I've been chained up for four months,' I railed at him. 'How do you think locking me up in this place is going to help? I need some free time. I need some time to myself!'

Gallagher agreed, the doctors conferred – they would let me out for a few hours before I was to return for further assessments.

But I didn't want to be probed or questioned any more, and I certainly didn't want the meds they wanted to put me on.

As I stepped outside for the first time on my own, I knew for certain I wasn't going back. As I walked to the main road to hail a cab, I passed a newspaper stand. The headlines screamed out: HORROR ON MARSHALL STREET; MADMAN'S SEX ORGY WITH CHAINED WOMEN; SEX SLAVES AND MUTILATION IN PHILADELPHIA.

My eyes flicked around the stand – Heidnik was leading on every single paper. I grabbed a copy of the *New York Post* and in the cab on the way to my old neighborhood, I skimmed the numerous pages devoted to our story.

The press had fallen on the gruesome details with all the delight of a dog devouring a bone: 'BODY PARTS FOUND IN PHILLY'S HOUSE OF HORROR' ran the headline. There were pictures of all of us in it. They were calling Heidnik the 'Rolls-Royce Reverend', a man into 'stocks and bondage'.

I shook my head – no! That's not how it was at all. He didn't chain us up for kicks, it was to stop us getting away. I wanted to call someone up, tell them their mistake and get it changed. I was angry and confused – my name and face were everywhere. I was suddenly public property. All I wanted was to get away from all of this for a few hours, to forget it all, try to put it all behind me. I knew where I was going.

We pulled up on the corner of Six and Gerard and I handed the cabbie a five-dollar bill, telling him to keep the change. On the corner was one of the dealers I was familiar with from my old life. I got a $100 bag of crack and headed to Marnie's, an old friend of mine.

I took the stairs to her apartment on the third floor and she greeted me with a generous hug. She was pleased I was okay but she didn't question me. I could see she was high and that's where I wanted to be.

'You got some gear?' she asked once I was inside.

'Sure,' I said. 'You got a cooker, lighter? I don't have anything on me.'

Marnie rummaged around in her pockets and pulled out the small bottle we called a cooker and a lighter. She went into the kitchen and returned with a small pot of baking soda and some water. I set to work pouring the powder into the cooker, adding baking soda and water.

Then I held the lighter underneath the bottle until it started to boil. At that point I stopped and poured in cold water, the powder now quickly turning into a rock.

I took it out and placed it in the pipe she'd given me.

Now I put the pipe to my lips, held the lighter over the rock and inhaled deeply – once, twice, three times...

Suddenly all the anxiety and tension I'd been carrying around with me melted into nothingness. I felt my arms and fingers slacken as the drug seeped round my body, stroking my limbs with a gentle numbness.

My head cleared of all the horrors and trauma I'd been

through the past four months – now I was floating on a sea of calm and euphoria.

I sank back onto the floor and surrendered myself completely to the drug.

* * *

I stayed with my friend a couple of days but then the media caught up with me. Someone walked in one day and said: 'Hey, you know Channel 6 are outside.'

So I took refuge at another friend's place. The problem was that the reporters had visited all the dealers and the hookers in the area, handing out cards and promising fat checks if they could find me. These were not the sort of people you could trust with a secret, not when there was money involved.

So it became a cat and mouse game between me and the press – forever being chased down from one apartment to the next, the reporters never far behind, always on my tail.

One day I got called into Gallagher's office. But when I stepped outside, it was raining. I was rooted to the spot, letting the droplets fall onto my head. I hadn't experienced rain in four months. I put my hands out now to catch the water and let it slide off my hands.

It seemed miraculous to me – incredible.

It was pouring now, coming down in sheets and running down my back, into my shoes and over my shoulders but I didn't care. I stood there like an idiot, letting myself get completely drenched.

Who would think you would miss rain?

I started laughing to myself, a crazy, stupid laugh. I felt ecstatic, elated, alive!

* * *

'The other girls have come to me with their lawyers – they told me they were considering filing charges against you.'

Gallagher was perched on the corner of his desk, looking at me intently. I'd changed out of my wet clothes to meet him and now I could hardly believe what I was hearing. The ecstasy I'd felt just an hour before at walking in the rain dried up.

I'd risked my life to save these girls and this was how they repaid me?

At first I was too dumbstruck to respond but finally I found my voice: 'Why?'

'They want to say that you were part of it, that you gave out the punishments because you liked it, that you were Heidnik's partner in crime.'

My fists clenched in anger. *How could they say those things?*

Gallagher could see my blood rising and went on quickly: 'But I told them: "Don't you realize that if it wasn't for Josefina none of you would even be here today? She saved your lives." Well, they thought about that and then decided they weren't going to be pressing charges after all.'

The betrayal was beyond my comprehension.

'Why?' was all I could manage. 'Why would they do that?'

Gallagher sighed and removed his glasses from the bridge of his nose, rubbing the place where they'd previously sat. 'You got to understand, Josefina, they've all got lawyers. They're all cutting up, wanting a bigger piece of the pie for themselves. I reckon they think they're going to get it too if they can put you in the picture with Heidnik.'

I'd been reading about Heidnik and his so-called financial wizardry. Turns out he had half a million dollars stacked up in an account in the name of his church, all thanks his astute investing on the stock market. That was how he could afford the cars.

My mind now turned over, thinking about the girls again. Heidnik had freed me, but only because I had signed his paper agreeing I was responsible for killing Deborah. Was that what this was about? I wondered about that time I'd gone down to the basement with Agnes. They'd looked at me then, looked at me as if I was a traitor. Didn't they realize now what I was doing?

'What about the piece of paper?' I asked Gallagher. 'Did you ever find that? The one he got me to sign about electrocuting Deborah?'

Gallagher shook his head.

'The police turned that house upside down but they never found it,' he said. 'And I don't expect them to. Heidnik more as likely got you to sign that paper just to make you believe he had you over a barrel. It was as incriminating to him as it could ever have been to you so he probably destroyed it pretty soon after you wrote it.'

I knew by now that Heidnik's lawyer, a man called Charles Peruto Junior, was going for an insanity plea. It was his only chance of getting him off the electric chair.

'… so it was only a matter of time,' Gallagher was still talking but now I'd lost the thread.

'Only a matter of time before what?' I asked.

'Before he got rid of you,' Gallagher went on. 'You were the only one that knew everything, you were the only one who could stand as witness to it all from beginning to end. He may have freed you for a while but it's clear he wouldn't have kept you around much longer. You got out just in time, in my view.'

It was all coming so thick and fast I was struggling to keep up. Something else occurred to me now.

'They put my kids' names in the papers,' I vented, angrily. 'Their names and ages and where Toya's at school. What's that got to do with anything? Why did they do that?'

'You got to try and ignore this stuff,' Gallagher said patiently. 'It is just par for the course. The media will print anything they can find out about you. You're the main prosecution witness. My advice is to stop reading the papers, then it won't upset you.' He changed tack: 'You ready for the preliminary?'

I nodded.

I'd been briefed about what came next – the preliminary hearing, just to see if there was enough evidence to take Heidnik to trial. In Gallagher's view, it was just a formality but it would be my first day in court. My first of many.

As I left the office that day, a woman passed me on her way in.

'Josefina!' she exclaimed.

'Lisa,' I responded. But neither of us stopped to talk, we both just kept right on walking.

Later that night I wondered why I didn't stop. We'd been chained up for months together in that basement, seen the worst horrors a person could imagine, experienced pain, deprivation and torture. We'd shared and endured the abuse of a cruel and heartless man, suffered his punishments, obeyed his every whim.

Now we couldn't face each other for a few seconds.

Did she want to talk to me, I wondered? I certainly didn't want to speak to her, not after learning about her betrayal from Gallagher. In that revelation I got the measure of the woman. I knew now that whatever I faced on the outside of that basement, I faced it alone. We may have kept each other sane during those months of captivity, helped and comforted each other during difficult times but now we were out, we were nothing to each other.

* * *

On April 23, 1987, a little under a month after my escape, I was led up to the witness box at City Hall to give evidence for the prosecution.

The charges read like the script of a horror movie: murder, kidnapping, rape, aggravated assault, involuntary deviate sexual intercourse, indecent exposure, false imprisonment, unlawful restraint, simple assault, making terroristic threats, recklessly endangering another person, indecent assault, criminal solicitation, possession and abuse of a corpse. I didn't know what half of these charges meant so I had to get the police to explain them to me. The last one was unlawfully treating a corpse in a way that he knew would 'outrage ordinary family sensibilities'. Well, he sure did that.

All of Heidnik's captives were there but we were kept in separate rooms before giving our evidence. There could be no possibility of our testimonies influencing each other. The press attention around City Hall was unbelievable – I'd never seen anything like it. It was a sea of cameras, reporters and media vehicles. They had to smuggle us in the side door. When it came to my turn to give evidence I was led down a long corridor into the courtroom. The first person I caught sight of was Heidnik – he was wearing a strange blue Hawaiian shirt and he'd clearly not shaved or washed since his arrest. He was already playing his 'insanity' card, I thought. Let him try it. Let him just try.

I wasn't intimated at all as I sat down to tell my story from beginning to end. I wanted them to hear the truth from my own lips, let them know what really happened.

Gallagher led me through my testimony in a calm and considerate way and after he sat down it was the turn of Charles Peruto Junior, Heidnik's defense attorney.

When Peruto asked me why I punished the girls as Heidnik directed me I explained in simple terms. 'He ruled all of us with an iron hand and he expected to be obeyed.

When he told me to punish them, I didn't even consider saying no.'

He asked me a few more questions – they were more like personal attacks than anything else. I glared at him from the box.

I was beginning to see what he was doing – trying to paint me as an accomplice. But it wouldn't work. How could it possibly work?

The next day the papers were filled with reports of the victim's testimonies – I bristled as I read the headline: HEIDNIK'S GIRLS.

It was a strange way to describe us, the victims. 'Heidnik's Girls' implied we had some choice in the matter. Until we were captured and held against our will, we were all individual women. Now we were Heidnik's, his possessions, just as he wanted all along. It made me mad as hell.

There were also some grisly accounts from the medical examiner who gave his evidence after me.

His description of what he discovered in Heidnik's kitchen certainly made for grim reading.

'Located in the freezer compartment of the refrigerator were several white... bagged parcels. As you would perhaps wrap up a piece of meat to keep it in the freezer, double wrapped in a white plastic bag. One of these bags had been previously opened. And I looked inside this bag and I believe I found two human forearms.'

He went on. 'In sum, there were two forearms, one upper arm. Two knees, and two segments of thigh. Each of these pieces had… the bone end had been cut apparently with a saw. And the skin and muscle, soft tissue, was still on the bone.'

The details were so gory and sensational, it felt like nobody could take this seriously. It was simply too horrific and so, in some twisted way, the press and the people I spoke to turned it into a joke.

Now when I saw old friends they usually had something smart to say about how they heard I was eating dog food and bodies.

I walked down the street and people actually wound down their windows to holler 'Alpo' at me. It was extraordinary and disturbing. Would they do that if I was their sister or wife or mother? I found it really strange that some folks decided to actually attack me for being a victim of a vile and cruel man.

Gallagher was sympathetic – he said all the other girls were going through the same thing and told me again to stop reading the papers.

I tried not to let it get to me – in my mind, I'd achieved the impossible. I'd escaped, so whatever anybody said to me didn't matter.

But when the whispers started behind my mom's back, I felt bad. She didn't deserve to be hounded by the press or the subject of unpleasant gossip.

Fortunately, Mom had a lot more sense than most people.

'What are you all whispering for?' she demanded to know one time on the bus when she overheard a pair of snickering ladies laughing and pointing to her from behind.

She turned to face them full on like a proud lioness ready to defend her cubs till the death.

'You think I'm ashamed? You think I've got something to be sorry about? My daughter got free of that madman and she saved the lives of them other girls too. I'm damn proud to call her my daughter. So you don't got no reason to whisper. Sisters – thank the Lord them girls are alive and pray you never have to face a madman like that Heidnik!'

And with that she stormed off.

* * *

Everyone had an opinion, everyone had their own ideas about what I should or shouldn't have done. I read something new and untrue in the papers every day. Now Vincent Nelson was claiming I was his girlfriend and that I went to see him before calling the police on the night I escaped.

'It's such bullshit!' I exploded at the cops one day when they'd called me in for about the millionth time to go over some small detail in the case.

'How are they allowed to keep printing all this stuff that isn't true? He was never my boyfriend! I don't know how this guy's gone and carved himself out some special place in this whole thing because he's got nothing to do with it!'

They were pleading with me now: 'Stop reading the papers. It will only make you angry.'

But it was too late. I was already angry.

* * *

My social worker came to me one day. Mr and Mrs Sepulveda wanted to adopt Ricky and Zornae. Would I agree?

With a heavy heart I said yes – I knew this was coming. From that first reunion in Gallagher's office I knew I'd lost them. I had only seen the kids a couple of times in the past few months and each time they seemed more and more detached from me. I didn't have the heart or the energy to fight for them. I could see they were a loving family and I knew it would only increase those kids' trauma to be unsettled from their lives again.

I signed the adoption papers without a degree of doubt.

The fact was, I wasn't really a good candidate for motherhood. I was using crack again, self-medicating I think they call it these days, and constantly moving from one friend's house to the next, staying on any sofa I could find, trying to stay one step ahead of the press. I still saw Toya every week and I would always be Mamma to her but Ricky and Zornae didn't know me at all. Was I really going to wrench them from the arms of the woman they knew as their mom to inflict on them a painful separation and adjustment? Did I even have it in me to be a mom right now?

Probably not.

* * *

Now I spent my life ducking out on all the people who came to find me. Even the detectives were a pain.

'Hey, Josefina,' said one dealer when I went to score. 'You know there's some detective looking for you.'

'Yeah, I know,' I said. What was wrong with these people? Couldn't they just wait a couple of days? I was sick of being at their beck and call the whole time. I wished everyone would just leave me alone.

The welfare payments weren't enough to sustain me any longer or pay for my drugs so within a few months I was back out on the streets, hustling. It was all I'd known for so long I couldn't think how else to cope. But it wasn't long before I ran into trouble again.

One clear, warm evening in July I was hustling on Front Street when a guy pulled up in a brown Ford. He was a fairly ordinary Joe in blue denim jeans and a lumberjack shirt, mousy brown hair and stubble.

We struck a deal and I got in the car. He looked normal – well, they all do. I wasn't really paying much attention when he stopped the car in a parking lot round the block but then he pulled out a knife about a foot long and told me: 'I'm Jack the Ripper!'

Oh Jeez! Here we go again.

I know what he wanted, he wanted me to be scared, but I wasn't. How could I be after Heidnik? I was just thinking – you can't be any worse than that nut so I shot back: 'Oh yeah? What's this all about? Huh?'

All the anger and frustration of the past few weeks now bubbled to the surface – *who does this creep think he is?*

I went on: 'I guess you just want some free pussy, right?'

Now he had his dick out of his jeans but I just kept right on talking: 'Well, you don't need that knife.'

I took his hand, still talking: 'If you're getting free pussy, I'm going to get something out of this too.' And I started moving his hand towards my crotch. He pulled his hand back in disgust. My forwardness has unnerved him.

'Hey, what do you think you're doing?' He seemed confused.

'You think you're the only one who's going to get their kicks tonight?' I was almost shouting now. I was furious. 'I don't think so!'

We were struggling now and he dropped the knife.

'Just get out of the car!' he yelled at me.

'Oh now you don't want to do anything?' I yelled back. 'What the fuck?'

'Get out!' he shouted again.

'Fine. Fine. I'm going!' and I slammed out of the car. Idiot! If he thought he could scare me he could think again.

I walked back up to Front Street and as I passed by the other hookers I warned them about the freak I'd just encountered.

'Brown Ford,' I told them. 'He's got a knife.'

'Thanks, honey,' they drawled back at me, most of them high. Would they even remember in an hour's time, when the night cooled down and they needed another hit?

I could have gone to the police that night and perhaps I should have but I didn't. He didn't actually do anything and besides, I felt stupid.

Mr Ripper turned out to be a wake-up call for me. If I was dumb enough to keep getting into strangers' cars, risking my life, after what had happened with Heidnik then I had no right to complain about the consequences. I could imagine walking back into the police station and telling them: 'Yeah, so I was just out Front Street and I met a guy with a knife who told me he was Jack the Ripper.'

'Oh, you again,' I imagined them laughing. 'What are you? Some kind of crazy magnet?'

And what would the press say? I worried that any bit of credibility I had would be destroyed by my reporting the man, which would impact on Heidnik's trial. In the end, I guess I was afraid that if I reported what had happened to me then the trial would collapse and Heidnik would basically get away with murder. No, better to keep my mouth shut and move on.

I had no right to complain. I knew better than anyone in the world there were crazies out there.

So I stopped tricking not long after. Risk and danger came with the territory and I'd had my fair share of that already. I had to find another source of income so by September I was working at a laminate company and still getting high.

At this point I didn't even consider giving up drugs – crack was the one thing that let me forget about everything. It held me at night in its warm embrace and let me sleep without dreaming, keeping all the bad memories at bay. Those memories came at me all the time, night and day, when I was least expecting it.

Occasionally I had an attack of fear so severe I didn't want to go outside at all. My heart raced, my head replayed all the terrible images I'd witnessed and I imagined Heidnik coming for me in the middle of the night. Even though I knew he was safely behind bars, I had a real fear that he would escape. At night I had to sleep with the light on because the dark brought such terror I lay on my back, paralyzed with fear.

The police still called me in every week and the psychiatrists were trying to help with the constant nightmares and panic attacks.

'We want to admit you for observation,' they'd tell me.

'Fine,' I'd say. 'But I'm not going on any medication. I don't want to be wandering through your corridors like another whacked-out zombie.'

'Then we can't admit you and we can't help you,' they'd reply.

And that was that – they left me to cope on my own. Which meant I bought drugs and got high. It was as simple as that.

Chapter Twenty-One

Limbo

If Heidnik was my captor and abuser, the man who haunted my dreams and cast a shadow over my waking life, Charles Peruto Junior was the one who buried me.

The son of a famous defense attorney, Peruto Junior seemed determined to use the Heidnik trial to get out from under his daddy's shadow, to make a name for himself

And he used me as a punchbag in court.

If I'd been Heidnik, I would have sacked him. Besides the way he treated me, I honestly didn't think he was a very good attorney. He had one idea and one idea only – blame Josefina Rivera.

His whole defense could be summed up in this way: Heidnik was too crazy to come up with the plan to capture and shackle a bunch of women in his basement or to invent the means of torture, it must have been me.

If he'd sat back and thought about that for any length of time he might have realized the ridiculous nature of the defense. You don't shackle your co-conspirator for more than 100 days!

But Peruto was so locked in to his idea he probably didn't properly consider the ramifications of his defense strategy.

At some point during Heidnik's trial, more than a year after our rescue, he actually asked the judge to instruct the jury to consider the possibility that I was an accomplice, something I didn't discover until much later.

It took the judge herself to point out the flaw in Peruto's logic.

'If the defendant is clever enough to enlist the aid of an accomplice, he knows what he's doing,' Judge Abraham told Peruto Junior. 'This could be a problem if you charge Rivera… If you want an accomplice charge I'll give you one, but Rivera is no fool. It is no great leap to say if your client got someone to work with him, if he's smart enough to get an accomplice, he's not insane. Why don't you talk it over with your client?'

In the end of course Peruto Junior dropped the idea of charging me too but that didn't stop him going after me like Rottweiler.

And the result of that was immense and far-reaching.

From the moment I came up against Peruto I become Josefina Rivera – Victim or Accomplice? It was too neat, too enticing for the press to ignore.

And so, whatever the outcome for Heidnik of his days on the stand, the writing was on the wall for me from the start. I'd lost my children, my freedom, my sense of self, a good part of my sanity and now I was about to lose my standing as a victim.

But this was all far, far in the future. For now I was stuck in an uncomfortable limbo, unable to talk publicly due to the. gagging order and yet still the subject of unending speculation. The press hounded me and my family, I was trying to keep up the pretense of a normal life but underneath I seethed, waiting and waiting for my time in court.

Neither the police nor Gallagher wanted me to read the press reports anymore – they thought it made me too angry – but I couldn't help myself. As much as I hated reading about myself, I was ravenous for more information on Heidnik.

From the moment he took me prisoner, huge questions haunted me. *Why did this happen? Who was responsible?* I'd worked out that I had my part to play in this and I'd heard Heidnik's reasoning but what was the truth?

I scoured the papers every day, searching for answers. There, I learned about Heidnik's strange and unsettling past. I read it all, desperate to understand more about this man, about what drove him to do the things he did.

I learned how he and his younger brother Terry were born to a violent father and an alcoholic mother in Cleveland, Ohio.

She, Ellen, was an attractive beautician with a Creole heritage and he, Michael, was a tool-and-die maker. Their marriage, by all accounts, was miserable. And the boys suffered too.

Michael was a harsh disciplinarian and didn't spare either child. He inflicted punishments so humiliating and terrifying that both children grew up hating him.

One punishment for Gary was being hung out of the window by his ankles, another included having a bullseye painted on the backside of his pants to show the other boys at school where to kick him.

His parents split when he was two and his mother went on in her shabby, chaotic way, marrying three more times before killing herself by drinking mercury in 1970.

Gary and his brother Terry had both been in and out of mental institutions for most of their lives, racking up a number of suicide attempts.

By the time of his arrest Gary had tried to kill himself thirteen times, including one occasion where he drove his motorcycle head-on into a wall.

It was fascinating but in some ways unsurprising – of course there had to be childhood trauma and dysfunction to create such a monster.

The stuff I found harder to digest centered on the agencies that frequently came into contact with Gary as an adult and as a direct result of either his mental ill health or criminal actions.

The two converged alarmingly in 1979 when he was put away for kidnapping Alberta, Anjeanette's sister.

One resourceful reporter turned up the old court files and quoted from a psychologist tasked with evaluating Heidnik in 1979 in connection to his conviction.

Astonishingly, the report predicted with alarming clarity Heidnik's likelihood of committing such crimes in the future.

The court psychologist wrote at the time Heidnik presented a 'high probability for serious or even bizarre offenses against relatively helpless members of the community.'

It went on: 'Of particular concern is the defendant's potential for engaging in sexually assaultive crimes against females.'

Heidnik, then 34, had 'engaged in a series of exploitative and manipulative relationships with a series of mentally retarded black women whom he may have exploited financially and sexually. This behavior seems to fit a pattern of taking an authoritative position in charge of more vulnerable individuals.'

He concluded: 'In order to avoid such a tragedy in the future it will be necessary for him to be very closely supervised and for him to receive continuing surveillance over a long period of time.'

Prognosis for improvement? 'Extremely grave'.

They knew! I realized with horror. People knew what he was capable of and they still let him go free. I boiled with rage – if they had these reports, why was Heidnik allowed to roam the streets, picking up women every day? Why wasn't he supervised as the report had suggested? This was written in 1979 when Heidnik was sent to prison for his seven-year term. He bounced between mental institutions for the length of his sentence before his parole finished in January 1986. Within a matter of months he had begun to collect women in his cellar.

Less than eight years after the evaluation, Sandra and Deborah were dead. Why didn't the authorities heed the reports and keep Heidnik under close supervision?

The judge at the time paid attention to the psychologist's warning and gave him the maximum sentence possible. But after that he was turned loose, free to torture, abuse and kill at will.

I read on. The psychologist, Dr Wayne C Blodgett, had been tracked down and told the reporter why he made such strong remarks.

'In this particular case, I just had a bad feeling about this person,' he said. 'I wanted to communicate that to the court.'

If only somebody had kept up close observation of Heidnik, as Blodgett suggested, two women might be alive today.

I wanted to hurry up and get to the trial. I needed to know more. I needed to know how Heidnik was allowed to fall through the cracks.

But the waiting went on.

Aside from the usual evidence-gathering that takes place before a trial, a major cause of delay was the fact that Peruto petitioned the court to move the case to a different city, on the grounds that there had been damaging press in Philadelphia that could prejudice potential jurors.

The judge denied Peruto's motion – she wanted to see for herself whether the ordinary citizens of Philadelphia had heard too many Heidnik horror stories to prevent them being able to make an objective decision in the case.

The question was not 'was Gary Heidnik guilty?' That had been established beyond doubt. Nobody could have argued that they'd got the wrong guy. The question now was whether he knew what he was doing when he did it. Was he insane?

If so, the charge would drop to second- or third-degree murder and Heidnik would be saved from the electric chair.

Peruto was hot on the insanity plea right from the start. He happily told anyone who'd listen that his client was 'out to lunch'. This was the main thrust of his defense.

I turned up to as many court hearings as I was allowed to attend. Many of them were the financial hearings. On one occasion, Peruto announced confidently, 'I am positive that any psychiatrist who examines Gary will conclude that he is suffering from a mental disease.'

He went on, 'When someone is dealing with him on a subject he's interested in, such as stocks and bonds, they may believe there is absolutely nothing wrong with him. But if you discuss a matter that is annoying to him, he is totally irrational.

'Gary has been abused so severely in the past that he may not even be responsible for his own predicament. Sometimes he doesn't even realize he is in jail.'

It took three days of trying to select a jury before Judge Lynne Abraham gave up and moved jury selection to Pittsburgh, a city far west of Philadelphia but still in the state of Pennsylvania.

By now I was staying in an apartment over the garage of my brother-in-law's place in north Philly where fortunately the press had failed to track me down. Angelo was married to Iris but they were in the process of separating and right now it seemed the only place I could move around freely.

It was Iris's idea.

'Listen, no one here is going to tell them and they can't connect the two of you through the records so take it,' she urged.

I did – it was my last refuge and sanctuary. I didn't even consider going to my mom's place – why would I want to bring all this down on her head? She didn't deserve it. Besides, Angelo had a habit too and he understood my need to get high.

The psychiatrists I'd been sent to were less concerned with helping me than hearing the story. I wondered how giving them the gory details was supposed to help me deal with the constant nightmares, panic attacks and anxiety.

One doctor even admitted in private, 'We don't know how to help you. All we can do is try various drugs. You girls, unfortunately, are the guinea pigs. Nothing like this has ever happened here before so we're doing the best we can but we're in the dark. We can try and then we'll know better for the future but right now, we don't have any miracle cure.'

In those early months after my escape I was given a place at a women's group home. The people were lovely but at night they wanted to turn the lights off.

'No, I'm not staying,' I told them.

Eventually, thanks to Mary's help, we came to a compromise – I was placed in a room on my own and given two bright night-lights. I lasted a week. The place was on continuous lockdown. I couldn't come in or leave when I liked. The restrictions were maddening and oppressive. I couldn't stand it – nobody seemed to understand that I was trying to recover from incarceration. How could locking me up again help?

Gallagher and the police also knew about my habit. I hadn't tried to hide it from them but I guess they thought it would be better all round if their star witness wasn't a crack addict, so a few months before the trial I was sent to a swanky upmarket center for drug rehabilitation. I didn't care one way or another and frankly I wasn't that interested in stopping but I went, just to appease them. The place was usually for wealthy people and the main house and grounds were amazing. There was everything you could possibly want or imagine – swimming pools, tennis courts, beautiful gardens, and great food.

But like with any rehab, they treated me like a child, telling me what I could and couldn't do. In the end, however you dress it up, rehab is a bit like prison and the staff are your wardens. They are there to stop you doing the things you like to do. The restrictions placed on me again were unnerving and the group therapy sent me insane. I had to listen to hour after hour of everybody else banging on about their addictions: what they took, how much, how it felt, what they did afterwards. After a couple of those sessions the only thing I could think about was drugs.

It didn't work – so here I was, back at Angelo's place, getting high, getting ready for Heidnik's criminal trial. The only thing that I could rely on to numb the intense pain and anxiety was crack. It was the only way I knew how. On the surface I carried on as normal but that was thanks to the drugs. At this stage I had no intention of giving that up. Crack had become my release and my sanctuary from the memories of the horrors I had survived, as well as the horrors I was going through since my release.

* * *

At the same time as the criminal case was under way, all the financial aspects to the case were being heard in the civil courts. Accompanied by my lawyer, I attended every single hearing. Joseph Grimes was one of the first lawyers brought in to speak to us victims. He was tall with dark curly hair and glasses and I found I could talk to him easily. He decided to take me on exclusively and was a tremendous support in those early weeks as the court system took over from the police investigations.

For the most part the financial hearings passed in a blizzard of legal jargon, much of which I didn't understand. But Joseph explained what was happening as we went along. And the matter became a fight over jurisdiction between the local and the federal courts.

I, along with all the other captives, was suing Gary Heidnik, as were the families of Sandra Lindsay and Deborah Dudley and the State for back payment of child support. Heidnik's accounts were frozen. Judge Samuel Lehrer in the Common Pleas Court was outraged that Heidnik had hidden his money in the church account, claiming the money wasn't his but belonged to the church. He accused

Heidnik of using a legal loophole in the tax system to evade taxes and described the church as a 'sham'. Heidnik filed for bankruptcy and at that point the Federal Court waded in, striking down Lehrer's judgment and assigning the case to the federal bankruptcy court. Now, we were told, the case would have to be wait to be heard in the federal courts. This would take some time.

Meanwhile, the funerals for Sandra and Deborah went ahead – I wanted to go but the police stopped me. 'It's not a good idea,' they told me.

I knew that my mom and Toya still endured whispers and taunts but neither of them got down about it; at least, that's what they told me. But inside I seethed. Why did they have to suffer? Mom was accused of raising me badly, that this was somehow all her fault. I was so mad I wanted to scream.

'You were the one who helped me survive this thing,' I told her. 'That's what you brought to the table. I was the one who was out there. I put myself in that position.'

'Listen, don't you worry,' my mom reassured me. 'I'm proud of you. I always have been. Nothing can make me feel bad about what happened.'

As the date of the trial approached, I became more and more determined to put the record straight. The week before it started Mary took me to the courtroom in City Hall where the trial was to be held. A once-beautiful building built some 100 years before, the old City Hall sat in the center of a traffic circle and though impressive on the outside, inside the huge corridors were dingy and depressing.

The lino floors were cracked, pockmarked and stained, litter was strewn about everywhere and there was a constant smell of urine leaching from the large stairwells. The place was so big there were courtrooms enough for eighty judges. We were assigned room 653 – this was where I was to give my evidence.

Mary pointed out the places where everyone would be sitting – over there is the defense table where Heidnik would sit next to Peruto, this is the prosecutor's table for Gallagher, over here is the witness stand where you'll be giving your evidence, the judge over there, and so on and so on.

I nodded mechanically, barely listening, trying to imagine what it would be like on the day itself. This was my chance to tell them the truth, tell them all what really happened. I wanted it so badly, but I couldn't help feeling a little fear, as much from the trial itself as what was to come after.

At this moment I couldn't see myself in the future or imagine what would happen afterwards. It was as if my life was on hold, just waiting for closure.

I was frightened of being met at the other end of this trial by that same void. What came after Heidnik? The trial and what had happened to me was defining my life right now, defining me. But what happens afterwards? As much as I wanted to know, I was afraid of the answer.

Mary was asking me now if I've seen enough – did I need to know anything else?

'No,' I told her. 'I'm ready.'

And I really was – ready to face the world, ready to face Heidnik again, ready to take on Peruto.

Chapter Twenty-Two
The Trial

I stood in front of the long mirror, eyeing myself critically.

It was Monday 20 June, 1988 and though there was a crisp chill in the air at this time in the morning, I knew in just a few hours the heat would be overpowering. So I had chosen a long sundress with large blue flowers and put on my best wig: long with tumbling auburn curls.

I tried to breathe normally but I felt a slight constriction in my chest. Today was the day I would give my evidence against Heidnik.

'Don't you worry about anything,' Mom told me on the phone the night before. 'You survived Heidnik, this here is going to be a piece of cake. Just get up there and tell the truth and don't let anything distract you from that. You can do this Josefina. Remember that.'

I recalled my mom's words of reassurance as I adjusted my dress and applied my lipstick: *You can do this. You survived Heidnik, you can do anything.*

It was Day 1 of the trial and I was the first captive to be brought to the stand. Before me, Gallagher would call up Sandra's mother to give evidence and then Officer Armstrong, who came to the house when neighbors complained of the smell but failed to discover us there.

I wanted to hear all the evidence but I wasn't allowed so I knew I'd have a few hours to wait in the morning.

Now I stood at the mirror, expecting the cops at any minute to pick me up for my day in court and I couldn't help feeling the huge weight of expectation and anticipation that had built up to this moment.

I was the prosecution's main witness. I had been told that. Of all the captives held in the basement, I was there the longest. Of all of us still surviving, I was the most articulate. If anyone was going to send Heidnik to the chair it would be me.

The next couple of hours went by swiftly. Mary met me at the house and accompanied me to City Hall. We waited in a small room for everyone to arrive – the jury, the attorneys and all the press.

Finally, it was time. I was led into a packed courtroom and the first person I saw on the table to my left was Heidnik, looking like a complete nut.

He was wearing the same Hawaiian shirt he had on at the preliminary hearing and I swear it looked like it hadn't been washed since then. He was there, but he was also absent, as if he didn't have a clue what was going on. I learned later he was doped up on Thorazine for the most part, but still, there was something vacant about him. His hair was wild and scruffy, his eyes stared straight ahead in a fixed, uncomprehending gaze and he didn't seem to be aware of anything around him.

Peruto, on the other hand, looked like a primped and preened poodle, his hair and beard neatly coiffed, his starched white shirt elegant and his tightly fitting suit bright and dapper. He seemed eager and excited, keen to get going.

I was led to the stand where I was sworn in and Gallagher got to his feet to start the questioning. I didn't stumble. I didn't get flustered. For three hours I slowly recounted the whole sordid story from beginning to end. Gallagher was amazing – he talked to me with a low, calm voice. His respect was evident.

By the time I'd finished the courtroom seemed baking hot. It was ninety degrees outside but thanks to a broken air conditioner, it felt even hotter inside.

It was Peruto's turn. I knew what was coming. I'd had a taste of Peruto's line at the preliminary hearing. He jumped to his feet theatrically. Everything about him seemed for show.

'Why did he say he was keeping you captive?' Peruto asked.

'He wanted us to have children,' I replied, but now my voice carried a hint of coolness.

'Why did he pick the cellar?'

'He said he didn't want to do it in the conventional way because the city kept taking them away.'

'How many women did he say he wanted and how many babies?'

'He wanted ten women to have ten children, all in the basement.'

Where was this going? I'd already stated all this in my previous testimony.

'He walked, talked and acted the same but what he was doing may not be what you would do, right?'

'Yes.'

Suddenly the penny dropped – he wanted to prove Heidnik's plan was so out there, so crazy, it could never have come from a sane person.

But soon Peruto switched tack – he went on the attack, accusing me of conspiring with Vincent Nelson to rob Heidnik before going to the police. Ridiculous.

I denied it.

He accused Nelson of being my pimp.

'I never worked for anybody but myself!' I asserted.

He then accused me of wearing a wig!

For a moment, I was thrown off guard. I could see what he was trying to do – cast doubt on my testimony, make me out to be a liar, someone who wanted to pull the wool over the jury's eyes. But I refused to be undone.

He asked me if I was wearing a wig today.

'Yes,' I told him honestly. I had nothing to hide.

Now this irritating and horrible little lawyer was really beginning to annoy me but I tried not to let him get to me. At least, not on the surface.

'Did you get any of your information from the media?' he asked.

'I was there. I don't need to get it from the media.'

He started trying to imply that once I was free I could have escaped at any time, that I stayed because I wanted to. I told the court again that my plan was to escape at a time when I could ensure the safety of the other girls.

There was silence for a few moments.

Finally Peruto said: 'Is it a fair statement that you would like to see the defendant convicted of first-degree murder?'

'That's right,' I shot back.

The judge ended the day's session before Peruto could get in any more of his pointless questions and I returned home that night, exhausted and agitated. The house seemed so quiet, I roamed from room to room, unsure what to do with myself.

Eventually, I made a ham sandwich and ate it in front of the TV. When Angelo got back from work we cooked up some crack and got high together.

I took the bitter-tasting smoke deep into my lungs, eager to let the drugs wash away all my tension and worries. It didn't take long. In a few moments I was back, floating on that cloud of happiness, drifting into another world where Heidnik and all the terrible memories of the cellar couldn't touch me.

But the next day I was back in the witness box and Peruto was going at me again, all along the same lines as the day before. He wanted to try and trip me up, get me to contradict my earlier testimony and admit to being complicit in Heidnik's scheme.

He asked if I'd been to a place called Carmesino's.

'No,' I told him. 'I don't even know what Carmesino's is.'

Apparently it was a place to buy cop stuff – uniforms, hats, and police gear. Next Peruto came at me: 'What if I told you I had a witness who saw you buying handcuffs in Carmesino's?'

'Then they must be lying,' I replied.

Now the judge spoke: 'Or mistaken.'

On and on it went – I wondered if Peruto was defending Heidnik or prosecuting me? The whole time he was on the attack, but he had nothing to go on so we kept returning to the same points over and over.

Eventually, I lost it.

'Is this all you've got?' I demanded. 'The same five questions? I've answered them all already.'

Judge Abraham waded in on my side. 'She's right, Mr Peruto. Get on with it – whatever you have to ask her ask her. If not, she's done.'

It was enough to silence him. Frustrated he sat down. 'Your witness.'

Gallagher rose slowly to his feet again. He had just a few short questions.

First he asked me what the first thing Heidnik did was after we got done dumping Deborah Dudley's body.

'He stopped to buy an *Inquirer* so he could check his stocks.'

Then he asked me if I knew where Gary got his ideas from.

'Yes – he got them from watching movies and TV. He got the idea of feeding us parts of Sandra's body from the movie *Eating Raoul,* and he got his ideas on punishment from *Mutiny on the Bounty.* He also saw *The World of Suzie Wong,* and he liked the way oriental woman were. That's why he picked a Filipino wife.'

After this I was free to leave the stand. I wanted to stay for the other girls' testimony but at the same time I wanted to get as far away from that courtroom as possible.

I felt a surge of good feeling. I'd done what I set out to do. I knew my testimony had been strong and that despite his best efforts Peruto had failed to rattle me.

No matter how he rephrased the words or sentences it was never going to change the basic fact that we were all there because of Gary Heidnik's bizarre ideas.

And two girls were not.

In all that time I spent in the witness box Heidnik never looked up, at me or even around at all the dozens of people packed into that small sweltering room.

Some part of me wished he had – I wanted him to see me, wanted him to know that I'd won. He knew how to work the system, that's what he'd told me time and time again and that was how he ended up fooling numerous psychiatrists into believing he was perfectly sane, when all the while he had naked women chained and starving in his cellar.

No, I didn't want him to get off on an insanity plea, that was true, because, knowing Heidnik, eventually he would have found a way to get out again and back on the streets. Heidnik had to be stopped once and for all.

He was too smart, too cunning to be let out ever again. If anybody could get out of prison after being sentenced to life, it was him.

So I knew he wasn't properly insane, not in the way the legal system defined it anyway. My lawyer had explained all the terms to me before the trial. A person who is legally insane is not responsible for their actions if, because of a 'disease of the mind', he does not know the 'nature and quality' of his acts, or doesn't know that those acts are wrong.

Gary Heidnik was not legally insane and I knew this because of what he did to the two bodies. With Sandra, he'd dismembered her body and tried to destroy the evidence because people knew they were linked and if her body was discovered, the police would come after him.

Nobody knew that Deborah Dudley was with him and they had no history together so he dumped her body whole in the wooded forests of the Pine Barrens. If they found her, it didn't matter.

He knew killing the two women was wrong but only one death could lead back to him so he used different methods of dispatch. If he didn't know he'd done wrong, why go to the trouble of cutting Sandra up into piece and hiding her in his freezer?

No, he'd approached these issues with his logical, cold and methodical mind. When he killed those women and got rid of their bodies, he was not insane.

I truly believed Heidnik deserved all that was coming to him – I knew that and perhaps he knew it too. The way he looked in court, it was like he was defeated already. My mind replayed our exchange in the house when I asked to see my family. Did he know it was all over then? When did he give up?

Not long after his arrest he tried hanging himself in the shower of the prison with a T-shirt. Another messy, unsuccessful suicide attempt. So perhaps he sensed the end was near, that he didn't deserve to live.

But he didn't deserve a lawyer like Peruto either.

In the end, the defense was based on a complete dead end – attacking the victims. Was that seriously going to help his client?

I didn't hear Jacqueline and Lisa's testimonies because they were on the same day as mine but I read the reports the next day that they didn't differ all that much in the details.

If I had been defending Heidnik, I would have tried to find out why he was even allowed to be walking the streets. It was obvious he had serious problems. Who was responsible? The army? The medical professionals? The criminal justice system?

Yes, I think I would have found a better place to point the finger than the victims. In the end it probably did his case more harm than good.

Chapter Twenty-Three
Heidnik's Mind

I returned to court on Thursday 23 June to hear the expert witnesses brought in by the defense. If my testimony had set the scene for the battle, the experts were to be the heavy infantry, fighting it out to decide Heidnik's mental state.

I wanted to hear for myself what they made of Gary Heidnik.

Peruto called up a psychologist, Jack Apsche. Apsche was charged with researching and evaluating Heidnik's mental health records. He had spent weeks wading through records in the States and Germany. Now he seemed ready to give his conclusions.

'In your opinion,' Peruto started. 'Did Gary Heidnik know right from wrong?'

'No,' came the reply. 'In my opinion he did not know right from wrong.'

'In your opinion, did he know the nature of his acts?'

'He did not know the nature of his acts.'

'Was he suffering from a mental disease?'

'Yes.'

'What disease?'

'Severe schizophrenia.'

Apsche went on to catalogue Heidnik's twenty-one admissions to mental health institutions, starting from his time in the army in 1962, when he was diagnosed as 'someone incapable of showing emotions and feelings and not having the capacity for interpersonal relations'.

The admissions stacked up one on top of the next – he complained of paranoia, hallucinations, delusions, depression and attempted suicide over a dozen times.

At one point he stopped speaking for two and a half years, claiming the devil had put a cookie in his throat.

'He did not say a word during that entire two-and-a-half-year period,' asserted Apsche. 'He engaged in non-verbal communication such as rolling up his pants leg. That was a signal that no one was supposed to talk with him, and he assumed everyone would understand that.'

At one point Apsche testified, when Heidnik was admitted to the Veterans Administration Hospital in Coatesville, he listed his race as 'black'.

I nearly fell off my seat! There was no one whiter than Heidnik.

'He was convinced he was black because his mother had told him so,' Apsche explained. It started to add up – maybe that's why he picked black girls for the most part. Did he think I was black too?

Peruto was trying to establish that Heidnik could not have been faking his illness, it was genuine from the start.

But when Gallagher cross-examined he threw doubt onto some of the specifics of Apsche's testimony. He contended that Heidnik had been faking all this time to collect his $2,000 a month in benefits from the Veterans Administration and the Social Security Administration.

The following day it was the turn of Dr Kenneth Kool, another expert witness for the defense, there to lodge the insanity plea firmly in the jurors' minds.

He was a courtroom veteran and his relaxed and easy manner suggested he was as comfortable there as the judge herself.

Peruto asked him if he had reached a conclusion based on the information.

'I don't know every element,' Kool began. 'But I have what I assume to be the highlights.'

'From November to March did he appreciate the nature and quality of his acts?'

'No.'

'He could drive a car,' said Peruto. 'Did that make any difference?'

'No.'

'If I told you that he placed a body in New Jersey, would that change your opinion?'

'No.'

Kool went on to testify that Heidnik was delusional and did not know it, that he was psychotic, he had an unbalanced perception of reality and his lifestyle was bizarre and regressed.

'What is a delusion?' asked Peruto.

'A delusion is an unreality perceived by the victim of it to be a reality.'

'Are you aware of his goal?'

'I'm aware of his delusional goal.'

Kool outlined Heidnik's grand plan, his 'partnership with God' to produce a whole community of children and described it as a 'fixed delusion'.

Did Heidnik know that what he was doing was unlawful, asked Peruto.

I sat forward in my seat. Now we were getting down to the crux of the matter.

Kool was unwavering in his conviction. 'He had some awareness of man's law, of what the laws of the Commonwealth were, but he saw God's law as superior. He did not have the capacity to reflect upon these things.'

This was news to me – in all the time I was chained up in Gary's basement, he'd never mentioned God to me once. It was Sandra who had told me he was the pastor of his own church. He himself made no reference to God or this so-called pact – and I probably spent a lot more time getting a feel for the mind of Gary Heidnik than any of these experts. So how was it the psychologists had this impression?

Kool was now delivering his testimony with quick efficient answers. Yes, he has seen a progression of illness from the medical records. No, he didn't believe that buying a copy of the *Inquirer* to check his stocks after dumping Deborah Dudley's body contradicted his assessment of Heidnik's mental state.

Peruto was trying to square Heidnik's apparent normalcy in some areas with his dreadful acts in others.

He got Kool to explain: 'His psychoses are primarily in the areas of reproduction – having babies and completing his pact with God. He does not have it in areas that are not conflicting.'

Yes, but did he really believe this pact with God stuff or had Heidnik just spun another clever story to snare the experts? I wondered.

Gallagher now stood to cross-examine the witness. He outlined Heidnik's pension-benefit history and asked if Kool believed the defendant had been faking it.

'No, he replied airily. 'In my opinion he has a major mental illness.'

'Do you think he was telling you the truth when you examined him?'

'Yes.'

Gallagher asked how he could be certain.

'I can't read minds. I'm giving you my best opinion. I can't tell if someone is lying.'

This was the defense case over. It was now time for the prosecution to bring out its big gun: Dr Robert Sadoff. Like Dr Kool, Dr Sadoff seemed relaxed in the witness box – I learned later he was a pro and had testified in thousands of trials for federal and state courts in twenty states.

His testimony completely contradicted Dr Kool's. According to Sadoff, Heidnik was a highly intelligent, calculating individual who knew what he was doing when he enslaved us all in his basement.

'The behavior that is on the record shows many indications that he tried to conceal what he was doing, that he did not want people to know what he was doing and that he had the intellectual ability and the awareness to know that what he was doing was wrong.'

Sadoff said a host of Heidnik's actions showed that he knew the 'nature and quality' of his acts and knew they were wrong.

He carefully planned the abductions, placed sound-absorbing tiles in the basement so we wouldn't know when he was home, mailed letters to Sandra Lindsay's family so they'd think Sandra was in New York and of course, disposed carefully of the bodies.

'Is it true that Gary Heidnik knew what he was doing when he picked up obviously mentally deficient girls and took them home to satisfy his sexual desires?' asked Gallagher.

'In my opinion he did. He is a man who has sexual interest and desires, and showed a plan of calculation and preparation. He didn't just grab them off the street.'

Sadoff delved into the details of the case. When it came to sending the letter to Sandra's mom he said, 'It's deceptive, it's calculating, it's premeditated – all the things that one has to have a fairly intact intellect to deal with.'

Even when bouncing from one mental institution to another, Gallagher pointed out that Heidnik had the wherewithal to always let his stockbroker know where he was, so he could send him his financial statement.

In summary, Sadoff asserted, 'Maybe he had a major mental illness. But the evidence indicates that he was not so deprived of his reason that he did not know the nature and quality of his acts.'

I found myself nodding along. I saw more truth in this than either Apsche or Kool's testimonies. The fact was Gary always boasted to me he knew how to work the system. If he didn't, how could he have kept collecting his disability check? He made damn sure he stayed in the easier mental institutions than spend any hard time in prison.

Sadoff concluded: 'There is nothing to indicate that Heidnik did not know what he was doing was wrong at the time he was doing it.'

A handful of prosecution witnesses followed – the dealer at the Cadillac showroom, an old girlfriend, and even a psychiatrist at a VA clinic who saw Heidnik three times during the period he had us all locked up.

In December 1986, while he had me chained and naked in his cellar, he kept his psychiatrist appointments and, according to Richard W Hole, showed absolutely no signs of mental illness.

'Mr Heidnik did not complain of symptoms nor did he show manifestations of ongoing or poorly treated schizo-phrenic illness.'

According to Hole, Gary's illness was under control.

'I asked him if he was depressed, and he denied that. I asked him if he was suicidal, and he denied that. I asked him if he was paranoid, and he denied that. I asked him if he heard voices or was having hallucinations, and he denied that. He essentially denied all psychiatric symptomology.'

If my opinion of psychiatrists was low before, now it hit rock bottom. How could a psychiatrist see him three times during that period and not get any clue that anything was wrong?

There was only one answer in my mind: Gary was a master manipulator. He was too clever to let the system beat him. He had proved that time and again. He'd ensnared two experts into believing he was so insane he didn't know what he was doing in his basement. If the jury believed them then Gary Heidnik would have won.

But Gallagher's troop of witnesses were compelling. And during this last batch, none seemed more devastating to the defense than Robert Kirkpatrick, Heidnik's stockbroker.

Interestingly, for the first time in the trial, Heidnik actually seemed to sit up and pay attention when Kirkpatrick was called to the stand. He testified that 'Bishop Gary Heidnik', as he always addressed himself to his Merrill Lynch stockbroker, was a very astute and shrewd investor with a flair for finance.

Heidnik had invested $15,000 in 1975 and by March 1987, the time of his arrest, he'd turned that into a $532,000 stock portfolio.

He usually kept in touch by telephone calls or through letters and Kirkpatrick read out excerpts from a couple of these.

In one he wrote: 'I saw that Tastykake hit 11 yesterday. I hope we got the 2,000 shares I previously ordered. Also,

I want to place an order of 1,000 shares of GPU at market. (Don't forget my 35 per cent discount.)'

On another occasion in 1983 he wrote: 'Please transfer our idle funds to our ready assets account. It should be around $16,000 and that's a lot of money hanging around not drawing interest. I remain respectfully at your service, Bishop Gary M Heidnik.'

'Did he ever lose money on Crazy Eddie stock?' Gallagher asked.

'No, he did not,' replied Kirkpatrick.

'What kind of investor was he?'

'An astute investor.'

It was then just a matter for closing arguments.

Peruto went first. 'The question is not whether Gary Heidnik did these heinous acts but whether or not he was insane. We're not contesting that these women were raped, that these women were kidnapped, that these women were killed. What we're here to determine is the level of culpability of the defendant. Even though we have conceded that these acts took place, we are not conceding first-degree murder – the specific intent to kill.

'Let's say he was a malingerer. A faker. That he went into the army with plans to develop a paranoid schizophrenic personality so one day he could make a living that way... Could he fool all those doctors all the time? Could he fake mental illness – schizophrenia – for twenty-five years? You have to believe that. You have to believe he did this for twenty-five years so that when he got caught building his family in the basement, he could say that he was insane. That's the prosecution's case. Does that make any sense?

'What was Gary Heidnik's purpose? His purpose was to raise ten kids, not to kill anybody. He was punishing the women for disobeying him, not trying to murder them. Third-degree murder is reckless disregard for human life. This is a classic case of third degree.'

On and on he went – at one point, in describing what Heidnik did with Sandra's body, he expanded in such grisly detail her mom started sobbing and had to be helped from court. He didn't hold back. He even pointed the finger at me, accusing me of 'feeding a sick mind', of going too far and even acting criminally.

It was enough to make me want to punch his lights out but I just sat there, stony-faced.

He sat down and we broke for a recess. Then it was Gallagher's turn.

He stood, folded his hands in front of him and started in his quiet, solemn tones: 'I want you to rely upon your good old-fashioned common sense. Rely upon your powers of observation. Go over the evidence with me.'

He turned and pointed dramatically at Heidnik, who had returned now to his old act of seeming completely out of it.

At this very moment he was staring at the rear wall.

'This man,' Gallagher's voice rose, 'repeated sadistic and malicious acts upon six victims. He planned it. He did it, and he concealed it. Ladies and gentleman, I submit to you – make no mistake about it – that this man committed murder in the first degree. It's clear that Sandra Lindsay and Deborah Johnson Dudley were killed as a result of being taken into that basement. It's clear that Gary Heidnik did it. It was premeditated. It was deliberate. It was intentional.'

Gallagher told the jury that none of the experts could read a person's mind, none could tell if a person was lying – the jury must rely on their common sense to deal with this.

'Just because someone does bizarre acts, the law doesn't recognize them as insane. What he did was premeditated, deliberate murder.'

Now he stopped still and looked intently at the jury.

'Reject this defense,' he said. 'Reject the very idea that this man is insane. Seek the truth, and I think you will find that this man, Gary M Heidnik, is guilty beyond a reasonable doubt of the specific intent to kill two young girls, and that when he did that, he knew what he was doing was wrong.'

Finally, the following day, Judge Abraham set out the charges to the jury in a lengthy address, complete with a green chalkboard, explaining all the legal language and the possible verdicts. They could find Heidnik either 'not guilty', 'guilty', 'not guilty by reason of insanity', 'guilty but mentally ill' or 'diminished capacity'. She also explained the various different degrees of murder.

It was lunchtime by the time she finished and the jury retired to consider its verdict. I didn't envy them their task.

The fact was, as much as I wanted Heidnik to go down, I wasn't convinced myself that it was first-degree murder. I didn't think Heidnik was legally insane – he was manipulative and deeply cunning – but to my mind he hadn't intended to kill either Sarah or Deborah.

That was what first-degree murder meant – that it was premeditated, intended murder. This wasn't Heidnik's intention – I knew that from first-hand experience. His aim was to father ten children. Why? Because I think he just wanted people around to love him. I think it boiled down to those very simple terms. In that respect alone, I agreed with Peruto. There was no motive to kill. He just never saw the consequences of his actions.

But with Heidnik we were looking at a whole different set of circumstances. On the last day of evidence the judge admitted a piece of evidence showing Heidnik scored 148 on the IQ test. That was intelligence at genius level. Could you ever allow a sadistic, evil genius back on the streets? Someone made the mistake once before and look what had happened.

If he was committed now, he would have to be committed forever.

No, it had to be a guilty verdict. Nothing else would work. Gallagher anticipated a quick decision but much to everyone's surprise, we had to wait two and half days to find out the result.

Chapter Twenty-Four
The Verdict

The word rang through the courtroom over and over again: Guilty. Guilty. Guilty. Guilty.

After sixteen hours' deliberations over two and a half days, the forewoman of the jury ran down the list of charges and repeated the jury's findings.

A wave of emotion swept through the courtroom – I saw Sandra and Deborah's families slump in relief as Heidnik was found guilty of all but one of the counts against him. Ironically, it was a charge of deviate sexual intercourse with me, which I had never fully understood since Heidnik certainly didn't have any deviate sexual preferences with me or the girls as far as I could make out.

But I too felt palpable relief at the outcome. After hearing all the evidence and the strength of the prosecution's case I didn't really see how they could come to any other decision. But they hadn't taken their duty lightly – they'd sat for hours discussing the case, which took just slightly over a week to hear.

Knowing that Heidnik would never be out on the streets again gave me some comfort, some peace of mind. Heidnik, as usual, was unmoved – he sat, bolt upright, facing the rear wall, jiggling one leg. His lawyer, however, seemed devastated. Peruto insisted that every single juror be polled and that's when we heard the word 'guilty' resound through the courtroom 216 times for eighteen counts. Peruto was utterly deflated.

But there was no celebrating. Just the task now of deciding Heidnik's fate – for the first-degree murder charge Heidnik could either be sentenced to life imprisonment or death. The next day the jury heard arguments on both sides and this time it took them less than two hours to decide. Heidnik was to be put to death for the murders of Deborah Dudley and Sandra Lindsay.

Judge Abraham thanked the jury 'for your service, not for your decision'. Then she turned to us, the victims.

'None of you girls are going to have to worry about him anymore because the next time Gary Heidnik sees the streets of Philadelphia he will be in a pine box,' she said.

Peruto had thrown himself forward in his chair and his head was bent onto folded arms. He was beaten.

* * *

As for me, I was still left wondering, even more so than before the trial, how this was allowed to happen. I wanted to be happy, I wanted to feel satisfied with the result but I couldn't help it. I was angry still. Very, very angry.

I headed straight to Angelo's place and obliterated the rest of the day in a fug of crack.

I had now been tarred by Peruto's accusations against me. He wanted to paint me as an accomplice in some way and though the jury rejected his theory, the media still enjoyed posing the question: Josefina – Victim or Accomplice?

I wasn't the only one who gave out punishments but during the trial it was never mentioned that it wasn't just me who was forced to do so. No one else was asked if they were victims or accomplices. In fact, totally inaccurate and damaging statements were made about me in the preliminary hearing in which it was claimed I beat the girls when Heidnik wasn't there. This claim was retracted at the trial and Jacqueline Askins reiterated that I did not give out any beatings except when Heidnik was present. But Lisa put the knife in on the stand, claiming that I enjoyed the beatings and that the electric-shock punishments were my idea. Why did she do that? I still don't know to this day.

For whatever reason, it only fuelled the public speculation about my part in the Heidnik affair.

I decided it was time to take the bull by the horns and accept an invitation to speak about Heidnik on the Wally Kennedy talk show.

I was there to discuss Heidnik's state of mind but of course I used the opportunity to finally have my say about my part. The rumors and gossip had gone beyond a joke – I felt like I'd been put on trial when all I'd done was escape and help free the other girls.

On the panel was a psychiatrist called Dr Clancy McKenzie, the first psychiatrist for the defense team who had nearly buried their case by his strange theorizing. So damaging was he to Peruto's case that Peruto himself had called him a 'flake' the day after he took the stand. He tried to distance himself as much as possible from McKenzie's testimony. Yet here he was again, outlining his idea that Heidnik's behavior was led by the part of his mind still trapped as a two-year-old.

'When he had to dispose of the bodies, it was like a two-year-old trying to hide the candy wrappers,' he said. 'He put body parts in a pot on the stove, in the oven, in the backyard, everywhere. The only thing he didn't do was run them up the flagpole. Do you know why he put body parts in the freezer? He was planning to start the babies – once they were off the breast – on human flesh. Infants suck for six months, and then they have a wish to devour the mother's flesh. This was the infant brain beyond a shadow of a doubt.'

I'd heard enough.

'Hang on there, doctor,' I interrupted him. 'Hang on a minute. I don't know any two-year-old who is sitting around chaining up his stuffed animals to a pipe or torturing them! His mind was way more capable than a two-year-old's or I would have been out of there a lot sooner!'

The talk show helped. From that moment there was a sea change in the way people approached me and talked about me – mainly to my face now, not behind my back. It was strange. I felt like a weird minor celebrity. Now instead of yelling 'Alpo' at me, people stopped their cars in the middle of the street to get out and approach me. Thankfully it was no longer to tell me I was a terrible person, but to say 'God bless you'.

The state of Philadelphia even presented me with an honorary certificate for helping to save the other girls and giving evidence against Heidnik.

I accepted but right now all I wanted was to get on with my life and try to move beyond Heidnik.

Chapter Twenty-Five
Moving On

'So what happened? Why didn't you warn me?' Deborah was mad.

'I tried, Deborah, I really did. You wouldn't listen to me.'

'You knew. You knew all along I wasn't gonna get out of there but you let me die, Nicole. You didn't even tell us your real name. You were never straight with us from the beginning. You gonna burn in hell, just like Heidnik.'

Deborah's eyes were dark black, her body seemed to swell visibly over me. Her movements seemed quick while I felt sluggish and slow.

Hot tears trickled from my eyes. I was sat in the hole, my legs shackled together, the cold damp soil all around me. I was naked and cold and now the hole seemed bigger and deeper than ever. She towered over me, from somewhere way up high. I was stuck down here, there was nothing I could do.

'You both killed me.' Her voice pounded down on me, filling the hole with her anger, her burning, seething anger. 'You and Heidnik together. You got no soul, Josefina Rivera! You could have tried harder. You should have done more. First you got rid of Sandra. Then you let me go. It's your turn next. I'm coming for you, Josefina. I'm coming to make you pay...'

Now the hole seemed to be growing and Deborah's voice was coming from further and further away as I sank deeper into the earth. The walls crawled with maggots now, creeping out of the dank soil, falling on top of me. The light disappeared as Deborah's dark form retreated and I fell down now, the bottom of the hole disappearing beneath me, enveloping me, burying me. I could barely breathe. I tried scrambling up the walls, which climbed ever higher, but with every movement I sank lower and lower.

'*HELP*,' I opened my mouth to scream but nothing came out. I couldn't hear my own voice, it was drowning in the vast cavern that had opened up above me. Now I couldn't even see the top anymore and still I was falling further and further. Desperate now, I clawed at the walls but the earth just came away in my hands, landing in soft lumps on my head, arms and legs. Soon I was swimming in a sea of earth and slipping down and down and down. The earth surrounded me now, up to my neck, soon it would cover me completely...

'*I'M SORRY*!' I tried to scream again. '*DEBORAH!! I'M SORRY!! DEBORAH!! DEBORAHHHH!*"

* * *

I woke with a start, my heart pounding – every inch of me bathed in sweat. My sheets were sticky, my neck ached. I heard myself panting.

My hands flew up to my face, my cheeks were damp too, but these were tears.

I was rigid with fear. Too scared to move.

I turned my head slowly to look over to my clock – it was 3:34 a.m. Now I was coming back into the present, reorientating my mind, replacing the nightmare with the reality of the here and now. Here was my chest of drawers with a picture of my mom and Toya lit by the bright overhead light that stayed on all night. Over there was my wardrobe, crumpled clothes spilling out the bottom, my shoes and sneakers lined up neatly by the door, my black jacket hung on the wooden chair next to my bed. I breathed slowly, trying to calm myself down.

You're not there anymore, Josefina. It's over.

The sweat was drying now, cooling my skin and tiny goose bumps broke out on my arms and legs.

For a moment I just held myself. It was the same nightmare I'd had since my escape from North Marshall Street. Always the same.

'Damn!' I said to nobody. It was a relief to hear my own voice. I tried to shake the fear out of myself, unsticking my body from the wet sheets. I tiptoed quietly to the bathroom and washed myself down, splashing cold water on my face over and over again, trying to erase the horrible memory of the nightmare.

I made myself a piece of toast and waited until it was light enough to take myself for a walk to clear my head.

I avoided the park, I still couldn't hear the sound of

leaves or twigs crunching under my feet without the fear of being out in the Pine Barrens with Heidnik rushing back.

At 7 a.m. the morning commuters were beginning to emerge on the streets, all brushed, washed and fresh for a new day. They looked determined, purposeful, as if everything in their life had meaning.

They walked briskly past me, sucking the wind along my body, reminding me of my crumpled, unkempt state. I wore just a grey, loose-fitting tracksuit, my hair pulled back in a tight ponytail, my fists dug into my black leather coat for warmth.

Eight years had passed since my escape from North Marshall Street and Deborah still came to me in my dreams.

I was haunted by the memories and nightmares of what happened to me in that cellar.

Night-times were the worst – mainly, I tried to avoid falling asleep at night so I stayed awake watching TV and caught my sleep in the daytime.

Thank God for Toya, who had started living with me again. Her presence injected normality into my life. I couldn't afford to lose it completely because I needed to be together enough to look after her. She was used to my strange sleeping habits. For the most part I was awake when she went to school and asleep when she came home.

If I got up and left the house early she knew why.

Toya and I had seen each other regularly since I returned from Heidnik's basement, then, when she was thirteen, I snatched her back from her dad. I had a feeling something wasn't right with her and when I insisted Ronnie take me over there to see her, I found out her father was planning to put her in a mental institution because she had memories of him snatching her the first time.

'There's nothing wrong with our child!' I shouted at him. 'How can you think to put her in one of those places? I've been inside a mental institution and it is the worst place you can imagine.'

With that I grabbed Toya and told her: 'Come back with me. You'll be fine. Don't worry about anything.'

Since then we'd lived together happily. I wasn't interested in having a relationship with a man. I couldn't even contemplate it. I was already dealing with so much.

The panic attacks were the worst. During lightning storms I became overwhelmed and couldn't calm myself down.

Nothing that anybody said got through. I shook and sweated, my heart zoomed and my mind raced at a thousand miles a minute.

I had no sense of reality and I didn't know what to do with myself. I was like a ball of pure energy, unable to walk, sit or stand in one place for even a few seconds.

I couldn't calm down. I was just out of it.

In those situations the only thing that worked was Xanax, an anti-anxiety drug.

The depression tended to come out of nowhere.

Suddenly, for no reason at all that I could work out, I wouldn't want to go on anymore.

I didn't see the point of getting up out of the bed, taking a shower or watching TV, cooking, eating or even drinking water. I didn't want to do nothing except hide in the corner or stay in the bed.

I felt hopeless and helpless. *Is this it?* I wondered. *Is anything ever going to get any better? The world is so full of nuts out to do harm. Am I ever going to have a normal life?*

In these bleak moments, I'd considered suicide but then there weren't any guarantees the next life would be any better than this one. Besides, Toya needed me. She was always in the back of my mind and then the inevitable sense of unworthiness descended. She deserved better than this. I wept for long periods. I didn't know if I'd ever stop.

Sleep came and went. No dreams now, no nightmares. No happiness, no sadness, just oblivion. I felt like I was nothing, worthless, weightless, pointless.

At some point during these periods, my therapist would be called. Somebody would dress me and next thing I knew I'd be sat in his office weeping again.

Then, through the talking, the cause of the depression would be discovered. I had been in a basement and that sparked it off. But now it was months down the line and I hadn't made it into work. So I would lose another job.

I was trying to get on benefits to cover my bills but welfare fought me all the way.

There's nothing wrong with you, they'd say. You could go out to work.

And it's true, for days or even weeks at a time, I could

be fine and then bang, out of nowhere, the darkness would descend and I'd be in bed crying again.

'It's hard to explain,' I told Mom after I lost another job.

'What's so hard?' she chastised. 'You survived Heidnik, you can survive anything.'

That was always her response. But it wasn't that simple. My year was now dictated by a calendar that I was always fighting and trying to ignore, but which engulfed me like a black cloud whenever November approached.

Thanksgiving, Christmas, New Year – usually such happy festivals for everyone else, but always for me, the anniversary of my capture.

One on top of the other, the seasonal holidays tumbled around me, a carnival of tinsel, carols and feasting. I didn't go out, I didn't celebrate. I stayed home and shut myself away.

The only place I felt safe was at church – there I was cocooned from the fears, the bad memories. I was comforted by God's presence. My faith was strong, I know that, but prayer didn't always bring the peace and serenity I sought.

The drugs had gone now. As soon as Toya came back to live with me I knew I no longer wanted crack in my life. For a long time it had helped me to forget, to bury all the bad stuff, but I knew that it couldn't go on forever. And once I'd made the decision it was, strangely, easy to stop. It was making the decision that was hardest. It took me a long time to find a place where I felt ready to let go of my crutch. I moved away from my old neighborhood, stopped associating with the old crowd and settled into making a life for us.

Toya and I had rebuilt our relationship and though I'd missed so much of her early life, I was determined to put things right and be the best mom I could be from now on.

I had lost Ricky and Zornae since their adoptive parents had moved out of the state but I had a chance with Toya now and I didn't want to screw that up.

Meanwhile, Heidnik sat on death row, awaiting the outcome of his appeals.

After all the fighting and the wrangling through the courts us girls got $30,000 apiece from Heidnik's estate. Most of the rest of the money went to the government.

Being out of work most of the time due to my depression and anxiety, I got through it pretty quickly – three years after the settlement there was nothing left.

I saw one psychiatrist after another – I was taught breathing techniques, prescribed tranquilizers, sleeping pills and anti-anxiety drugs. Sometimes they worked, sometimes they didn't.

It was Mom who was most concerned about me.

I went to see her once a week and, though now in her late eighties, she was still as vigorous and active as ever. Last year she'd been awarded the honor of Volunteer of the Year. Today she was making cakes for the senior citizens she visits.

'Are you happy, Josefina?' she asked, whisking a large bowl of gooey dough.

'I'm happy enough, Mom,' I said. 'Who's happy these days?'

'I'm happy,' she replied, pouring the mixture into one of her large baking tins. Then she put the cake in the oven, banged the door shut, and went over to feed her little potbelly stove with wood.

She was always busy, always on the go.

'I don't know, honey,' she said, poking at the logs. 'I worry about you. Am I ever going to stop worrying about you? You need to settle down, put down some roots.'

'Yeah, Mom, but I got to meet someone first!'

'You meet people all the time,' she said. 'You just don't want to get into it with anyone.'

She was right. How could I explain the nightmares, the depression, the strange fears to someone I'd just met? Who would want to put up with that? It was hard enough trying to deal with it all on my own.

Mom had now straightened up, putting her hand against the flat of her back where it ached, and letting out a quiet 'ooof', her eyes shut against the pain.

She walked slowly over to the porch and pulled out a couple of pairs of shoes, one pair in each hand. She was wearing a cotton peach dress with sunny yellow blooms and wanted to know if either her red shoes or black shoes went best.

'Mom, you're eighty-seven!' I burst out laughing. 'No one cares if your shoes match your dress.'

'Yes, well I care,' she replied prissily. 'Now, you tell me – red or black?'

Later, as I was leaving she took me in a tight embrace.

'I don't want to worry about you forever,' she whispered. 'Find someone nice. It's time.'

Chapter Twenty-Six
Recovery

In 1998 I met Theron. He was kind and funny and he offered me a new life in Absecon. Now I was ready to move away from Philadelphia, to try to put the past behind me. Mom seemed happy when I told her I was to marry again.

'At last I can stop worrying about you!' she smiled.

Theron and I moved into a hotel in Absecon – it was meant to be temporary accommodation but we ended up living there full time. It was a cheap way to live – for $150 a week everything was included, electricity and towels and housekeeping.

Theron was out of town a lot – he was a travelling salesman – and I worked in housekeeping at the Tradewinds hotel and also held down a job waitressing in Denny's restaurant. Toya had grown up and moved out by now.

I couldn't say I was happy exactly but I was content. I didn't think about Heidnik much and out of town, people didn't recognize me either. I was trying to make a life for myself. Theron didn't want to know about the Heidnik thing so I didn't talk about it much.

A year after we got together, in 1999, the state finally executed Heidnik. He didn't want to appeal but his estranged daughter had put in one last appeal for a stay of execution. I heard on the news that morning he was due to be killed and by the time I got back in the evening, it was done. There was no resistance, no last statements. He'd spent the day listening to country music then his last meal had been two slices of cheese pizza and two cups of coffee. He went willingly, peacefully to his death. Deborah and Sandra's sisters had attended, all dressed in white T-shirts with images of their dead sisters on them, and according to the news reports, they'd applauded when it was announced that the lethal injection had been successful. Well, that was their right. Neither Deborah nor Sandra had not gone willingly or peacefully. At 10:29 p.m. on July 6 Heidnik was pronounced dead. It was over. Well, it was over for him anyway.

If there was one thing I knew after all these years it was that it would never truly be over for me. I was bitter and angry about that. He'd got what he wanted all along – the oblivion of death. There was no sense of relief for me. From that night onwards I now feared his children would track me down one day – or perhaps that Heidnik himself would start haunting me.

My mom died a few years later – I'm glad she got to see me married because she always told me that she was tired of worrying about me. She was 92 and still her mind was as sharp as a knife when she died.

On my last visit I sat at her bedside with my adopted sister Althea and we all talked and joked together like old times.

Mom was so special – I worried I never told her enough. Through the years I'd often said to her: 'Mom, I love you.'

And her reply was always the same: 'Why, thank you!'

She was just so grateful be loved.

It makes me smile even today when I think about that.

But I don't think she ever realized how attached I was to her. She was my whole world. It was just her and me. She taught me everything and I valued everything that she taught me.

My sister Iris passed away shortly after. The poor woman lost her ever-loving mind. For a while she had cleaned up – she'd contracted HIV through needles and I think that shocked her into turning her life around. She went through rehab, got into the church and became a ministry evangelist. She preached everywhere – rescue missions, shelters, and people's homes. She really tried. Sadly, it didn't last. She began to get the cravings again and in one conversation when she was really struggling she told me, 'Honestly, Josie, I'm just sick of taking all them medications. It's making me sick. I just want to go the way I want to go.'

I pleaded with her, tried to help and inspire her. By now I was running a daycare from her house in Absecon and I told her she could come and help out with the kids, teach them Bible study, but it was no good. The lure of the drugs was too strong.

The next time I saw her it was with a bottle of vodka in her hand. Next thing I knew she was inviting drug dealers into the house so I had to close the daycare.

From there on, it was a fast ride down for Iris.

I was still working two jobs but Iris just filled her home and life up with dealers, drink and drugs and stopped taking her meds.

In a matter of months she was in hospital and weeks later she passed away from pneumonia.

She didn't care by the end – she knew she was going to die so she did everything she wanted to. It was sad, but it was also inevitable. I just hoped she enjoyed those last months because for us, her family, they were hell.

Theron and I didn't last. I don't think I was ever truly in love with him – he had just offered me another kind of life and that suited me at the time. We didn't share any special chemistry and as our marriage slid away from us, neither of us seemed willing to try and rescue it. We were married in name only – really, we were only just friends.

So it came as a complete surprise when I fell in love with my best friend. Chris and I had met through mutual friends in Absecon while he was going through a messy divorce. I suppose by now I had accepted my marriage was over but with Chris, he was all over the place.

We seemed to connect right from the start and I counseled him about handling his crumbling marriage.

They tried a reunion; it didn't work. Chris and I took long walks and talked about everything. For the first time in my life I was talking to someone very openly about everything I'd gone through with Heidnik and all the stuff afterwards. Chris didn't judge me, he didn't try to get me off the subject, he just let me talk.

It felt like we'd known each other for years.

'You know, I wish I'd met you a lot sooner,' I told him one day.

'Yeah, I think maybe that would have been best,' he said.

We both knew where this was heading and for the first time, I felt confident and safe enough to let myself fall in love.

By now Toya had kids of her own and we saw them all the time – my grandkids were crazy about Chris and it made me happy to know I'd found a man who loved my family too.

The problem was his family wasn't too keen on me – they didn't like the fact that I was Hispanic since Chris was white.

It seemed amazing to us both that in this day and age racism could still influence people's views and judgments, even when it came to their own family.

So in 2010 we moved away from Absecon and down to Atlantic City, near the sea. I loved the place right away – it was just the right size for me to walk around and being near to the water's edge always made me feel connected to nature.

I'd spend hours wandering up and down the beach, just watching the white crest of the waves wash up and down the shore. That great expanse of ocean made me feel safe, reassured. It was a world away from the darkness and confinement of the basement, the hole, which still haunted my dreams.

Freedom – I treasured that above all things. Once you've been locked up and kept away from the world the fear of it happening again is strong and real. Out by the sea, I felt I could always be free.

And it was here, in Atlantic City, I finally started getting the right kind of professional help. I met DJ, who also happened to be a pastor at my church, and with his amazing help I started to really tackle the demons that had haunted me all these years.

For so long I'd continuously blocked out what happened and put it on the back burner.

Deborah's death had haunted me for years – she came to me in my dreams a lot and I agonized over whether I did the right thing by her.

It always ate at me that I never took the time to talk to her a little more or get her to understand – then maybe she would have calmed down and it wouldn't have got to the point it did.

It was DJ who helped me get the correct diagnosis of Post Traumatic Stress Disorder and it was him who helped me to realize that the situation was really out of my hands: I had to stay focused or I would never have survived.

And there were other questions about Heidnik that I needed answers to, like who was responsible for the way he was?

If I ever met a member of the military, I'd always quiz them about getting disability benefit from the army. How difficult is it to get an honorary discharge with 100 per cent disability pension?

The answer was always the same: near impossible!

You could serve for forty years and get your legs and arms blown off and still not receive 100 per cent disability. It never came out in the trial because the judge refused to admit any speculative evidence without proof but I am convinced Gary was right about one thing: they must have done something to him in the army or why give him 100 per cent disability after just four months? It didn't stack up.

And yet without that money, Gary would never have been able to operate in the way that he did. It enabled him to enact his sick ideas.

After that all the agencies failed – the justice system, the mental health system and the military too. He slipped through the cracks, and it worries me that there are probably others out there today who may have slipped through too.

For the first time I was tackling these questions head-on instead of running away from them. It had taken over two decades but I was finally ready to sit down and analyze my time in the cellar, tackle my feelings of guilt and pain and make peace with the past.

Chapter Twenty-Seven

Reunion

'Mom, Mom!' LaToya's voice was breathless, excited. I took the call on my cellphone as I was coming home from one of my appointments with DJ and had chosen to walk along the beach. But I could barely hear her over the roar of the waves.

'Yeah, honey. What's up?'

'It's big, Mom, real big!'

'Okay, okay,' I said, my stomach flipping over. 'Just give me a minute.'

I ran over the dunes and onto the boardwalk then dashed behind one of the casinos to shelter from the wind.

'Okay, I can hear you. What is it?'

'Mom, it's Ricky. He got in touch with me. He found me on Facebook.'

'What? Our Ricky? My Ricky?' I was stunned.

'Yes!' She was laughing now. 'Can you believe it? We've been looking for them all this time and they've been looking for us too! He sent me a message. I'll read it to you. Listen to this: "Hey, my name is Ricky Sepulveda, formerly known as Ricardo Rivera. I think you might be my sister. My mom's name was Josefina." Can you believe that? Ricky's with Zornae and they want to meet us!'

I couldn't help it, I started to weep. It was the answer to our prayers.

For so long Toya and I had been searching for Ricky and Zornae but we had no way to trace them and when we talked to child protective services they told us they couldn't help.

Toya was desperate to meet her brother and sister – she had such clear memories of Zornae: pushing her along in her stroller, feeding her yoghurt. And it was Toya who had given Ricky his name.

We'd been watching an episode of *I Love Lucy* one day when she'd turned to me and asked me to name the little boy Ricardo.

Now, in November 2010 they had found us!

'Oh Toya, that's wonderful!' I said. 'Where are they? What are they doing?'

'They're out in Florida. They want to meet us.'

My heart was now going a million beats a minute and something occurred to me.

'Do they know, Toya? I mean, have they been told?'

'Don't worry. They know everything, Mom. Ricky told me their parents kept a cuttings file on Heidnik and the trial. They figured one day they'd need to know. So it's okay, they know everything.'

I clutched at my chest in relief. I'd always hoped one day I could meet my two children but the thought of telling them how we came to be separated was terrifying. Thank God they already knew.

That night I went home and told Chris everything. We both sat there afterwards, in shock, the silence occasionally broken by one of us exclaiming: 'I can't believe it. It's unbelievable.'

I didn't sleep a wink that night, too excited and too full of questions.

The next day we went to an Internet cafe and I looked at all the messages from Ricky and Zornae on Toya's Facebook page.

Zornae had written: 'I'm so excited to meet you at last. I just hope we can find a way to be together.'

My heart swelled with sadness. I'd missed so many years with my children – who were they? What were they like? I didn't know.

Toya seemed overwhelmed – by now she had settled down into a very secure and happy home life with her husband Russell, who owned his own property business and was a deacon at his church.

They lived in Texas and had four beautiful children all doing well at school – now, to learn that Zornae also had a little boy was thrilling. Toya was an aunt and she couldn't wait to meet her nephew.

'Mom, all this time we had family and we didn't know them,' she said on the phone that night. 'Now we've got a chance and we've got to take it.'

But how?

We couldn't afford the airfare to fly out to Florida to meet them and Zornae and Ricky weren't rich either.

In the end it was Zornae who came up with the idea of taking our story to a local radio station that ran a special Christmas Wishes Competitions. She called the station and explained our story – would they help us to come together for the holidays?

The station thankfully agreed to make us their special story for the Christmas holidays and provided the airfares so that Ricky and Zornae could fly from Florida to Texas and fly Chris and me from Atlantic City to meet them there.

We were all due to be reunited on Christmas Eve. It seemed so appropriate. Now, for the first time in twenty-five years I was excited about Christmas. It would be the best Christmas ever, in fact.

* * *

Sitting on the plane, sipping my water, I let my eyes roam over the clouds below. I was so excited, I could hardly sit still. I'd seen their pictures, I'd spoken to them on the phone and now it was time to meet them in person. Ricky and Zornae – the two children I'd given up over twenty years ago.

I recalled the moments I'd shared with them two decades earlier – the hugs, the kisses, the warmth. Did they remember any of that? I hoped they'd had a good life. I'd trusted the couple who'd adopted them – I wondered what I could offer them now.

I turned to Chris. I didn't need to say a word – he could see my anxiety, my worries.

'Don't worry,' he soothed. 'It'll be fine. Just try and relax.'

Chris knew me so well – he knew exactly what to say and how to handle my volatile moods.

DJ was there for me too – he'd given me his home number over the holidays, in case I needed to call him. He knew this was the right thing, a way to heal the parts of my past I never could on my own. But how could I tell them why I'd given them up? They understood what they'd read about me but they didn't know anything about the real Josefina Rivera. I was just a dream for them. An idea. A fantasy. It was like the first time I'd met my own father. I had prepared myself for the worst so it was a nice surprise to find him alive and well. But after that I had to adjust to the fact that he was a real person, with flaws and problems just like anyone else. I knew I could never match up to the fantasy these kids had built in their heads about me but I hoped that we could accept each other on new terms, as adults. As real people.

Chris and I came off the plane and he held my hand tightly as we walked through the Arrivals doors. My heart was zipping along at a million beats a minute. They had arrived three days before and were already staying with Toya and her family. Now it was my turn to meet them.

The first person I saw was Zornac – she was the spitting image of me!

At first I could hardly believe it was her – I'd left a tiny, skinny toddler who was struggling to get her weight up.

Here was a fully grown woman with curves and full sensual lips, like my own. She was clutching the hand of a little boy, Gary, her son. It was ironic that was the name she had chosen, but this little boy was nothing like his namesake – he was a complete angel.

Behind Zornae was Ricky, a tall, thin handsome man wearing a sky blue bandana. I could see his high cheekbones matched my own while designer stubble outlined the contours of his chin and lips. His eyes were deep and soulful.

'Oh my God!' I exclaimed, clasping my hands to my mouth, tears freely running down my cheeks.

'Mommy!' Zornae reached out towards me and we fell into each other's arms. Ricky then came up beside me, a shy smile playing on his lips.

'Mom?' Now I flung one free arm around his neck and the three of us stood there like that, hugging and crying for I don't know how long.

After all these years and all this time I felt truly blessed to have my children back in my life.

But right behind them a camera crew jostled to get the shot of us together.

'What are they doing here?' I turned to Chris. He shrugged.

Zornae spoke. 'They're from the station. They wanted to get the whole story.'

It put me on edge – although I was grateful to the station for bringing us together, I didn't want them to capture my most intimate moments of reconnecting with my children.

'Let's go,' I told Toya and she nodded, picking up my suitcase. We all piled into her car with myself, Zornae and Ricky on the back seat, little Gary sitting on his mom's lap.

He was just eighteen months old at the time and he kept looking between the two of us with a mixture of confusion and curiosity.

'He can see we're related!' I laughed. 'Smart boy!'

When we got into Toya's house, her kids were all there – LaQuoia, Bryahna, Jaaqwan and Sean – and we all hugged and kissed. The place was decorated like a winter wonderland for the holidays with tinsel everywhere, spray-on snow frosting up the windows and a great big tree with sparkling lights and dozens of presents underneath. I'd never seen so many gifts!

'Have you gone crazy?' I joked with Toya and Russell. 'Them kids are going to be so spoilt!'

'It wasn't us, Mom.' Toya shook her head. 'The station gave us a ton of presents for the children. We've been completely overwhelmed by their generosity.'

We enjoyed a noisy, boisterous meal with all the kids competing to fill us in on all their latest achievements but after we'd settled them down for bed it was finally time to talk with Ricky and Zornae.

'We have so many questions, Mom,' started Ricky.

'Well, shoot!' I said. 'I don't have any secrets. You know all about what happened to me with Heidnik.'

'I know. But there's so much I don't understand,'

he went on. 'Like where we were in all of that and what happened with us?'

'What do you mean?'

'Well, why couldn't you come and get us after you got freed?'

'Yeah,' Zornae chipped in. 'At first they put me in this foster home and I hated it and I kept thinking that eventually you and Toya would come back and get me but you never did.'

Oh God! The hurt went very deep here. For the first time I really began to see the reality of what these kids had been through and it made me feel so ashamed.

'I'm so sorry about the past,' I told them both. 'I was a mess. The Heidnik thing wasn't just like something that happened and then stopped. It gave me some serious issues to deal with, which I'm still dealing with now. I'm in therapy and it's very good but at the time, they didn't know how to help us girls. They just wanted to dope us up. The way I coped was the only way I knew how at the time: I took drugs. I'm not proud of that and in the end it hurt me more than it helped me but in the immediate aftermath, I had nothing else.

'I've got Post Traumatic Stress Disorder you see – they didn't even have a name for it back then. These days we know all about it because of the veterans coming back from war but it was pretty new in those days. I'm getting the right help now but I swear it's only in the last few years, and with Chris's help, that I've started to get things under control. I wasn't in a fit state to be your mommy back then. But I wanted to do the right thing by you, give you the best chance possible, and that's why I let the Sepulvedas adopt you.'

There was silence.

'But what about Toya?' Zornae asked.

'What about her?'

'She got to stay with you.'

'Is that what you think?' I was confused. 'Toya didn't come and live with me until she was thirteen. Until then she lived with her father.'

'Well, why did she come and live with you then and we couldn't?'

'Zornae,' I said slowly, trying to make this as easy as possible for her. 'You were adopted by then. I didn't have any say over your future. Toya and I have been looking for you for years but the child protective services refused to help because once you've given a child up for adoption, that is it. It is then the child's decision if they want to know you. I couldn't intrude or interrupt your life. That would have been wrong.'

Ricky was looking thoughtful. I could see he had a lot of my strength and independence – yes, he was a Rivera, through and through.

'What about our father?' he asked.

'Yes, well your father had a lot of children,' I said. I wasn't going to sugar-coat the truth. They deserved to know everything. 'He liked women, he liked to fight and drink and he wasn't the greatest candidate for fatherhood either. By the time the question came up, he wasn't really in the picture.'

We talked for hours that first night. Nothing was off-limits. I wanted to be as open and honest as possible so we got off on the right foot. No secrets. They told me too about their upbringing – some good, some not so good.

As the night drew to a close I wanted to say one final thing. 'Look, I can't change the past. It's done with. We've got to start from here, move forward in a positive way and look to the future. Whatever hang-ups you have about the past, you got to try to let them go for all our sakes. I know it's hard. I know I did things wrong and for that I'm truly sorry but I can't undo what's happened. I can only try my best from now on and if that's okay with you then I'd really like to try.'

Ricky nodded and then stood up to hug me. Zornae started to cry again and held my hand.

'I just want to be close to you, Mom,' she said in a little-girl voice. In that moment I saw them both as they used to be as little kids. I could see the babies I'd left behind.

'I love you, Mommy,' she said.

'I love you, Mom,' Ricky echoed.

'I love you too,' I said, and then I pulled them both back to look at them. What beautiful young adults they'd grown up to be!

'I'm here now,' I told them. 'I'll always be your momma, no matter what. Now, kids, I think it's time for bed!'

They smiled a little then and we hugged and kissed goodnight. It had been a tiring day. Tiring but utterly beautiful.

The next day was Christmas and the house buzzed with happiness and activity. Toya cooked up a fantastic turkey dinner and all the kids ripped into their gifts with breathless excitement. It was the best Christmas I'd ever had.

There were snowstorms in Philly that year but in Texas we were all dressed in shorts and little T-shirts thanks to the warm desert air.

Later we all went outside to play a family game of basketball.

I got teamed up with all the grandkids while Zornae, Ricky and Toya played on the other side. I tried to rally my team but it was completely unfair and we laughed hysterically as the little ones tried unsuccessfully to get the ball off the other team.

'Come on, Bryahna!' I urged. 'Get them!'

The kids screamed and squealed with laughter. Toya, Ricky and Zornae's faces shone with effort and exhilaration. We could have been any family, right then. Any ordinary, wholesome family just enjoying each other's company for the holidays. It was the happiest I'd been in a very long time.

We stayed just a week but it was long enough to get to know my kids a little – Zornae was basically a momma's girl, just like I had been with my mom. She always wanted to be by my side and was even a little jealous if I showed the other kids more attention than her.

Ricky was a headstrong, independent man with a fiercely ambitious spirit – he wanted to break into rapping and when he gave me a demonstration, I thought he was really good. He would succeed in whatever he chose to do, I could see that.

When Chris and I got back to Atlantic City, Toya was thrilled to announce that Zornae wanted to come and live with her. For Toya, it was all her dreams come true.

In fact, both Ricky and Zornae stayed on with Toya for a good few weeks afterwards. It meant so much to them both to reconnect to their family and I was pleased for all of them. After all, I wouldn't be around forever. Now they had each other and nobody could take that away.

As for me, I was simply grateful to have the opportunity to build a better future with all my children.

Epilogue

My favorite holiday is the Fourth of July, Independence Day. It means something to me. Around here they set off a load of fireworks along the beaches from Margate to Ventnor and Brigantine. But the Atlantic City fireworks are always the best. I guess it's because this is a holiday town and the big casinos like to put on a good show for the tourists.

Chris and I usually go to the beach and watch them exploding through the sky, lighting up the night in a brilliant display of color.

Last year we took a Ferris wheel ride on the boardwalk just as they were setting off the fireworks all along the coast. As we reached the crest of the wheel we saw a hundred fireworks streaking through the dark skies, cracking and banging all around us, for twenty miles down the beach. All the fireworks displays were being set off at once and we had the best seats in the house!

It was exquisite and extraordinary. I screamed and laughed and applauded like a little girl. The rockets fizzed upwards, leaving a sparkly trail in their wake before erupting into bright glitterballs of light. The shimmery confetti burned in the sky, fountains showered silver, red and gold sparks while cracks, whistles and fizzes broke out all around us.

Chris sat next to me, holding my hand, grinning away.

'I love to see you like this,' he whispered in my ear.

'I love to be like this,' I told him.

And it's true. I like being happy. I try to see the good and positive in most things and people. After all, we only get one shot on this earth and we've got to make the best of the cards we're dealt. So when I find pleasure and happiness in my life, I grab it with both hands.

My grandchildren now are my biggest pleasure – they are all such good kids, well mannered, smart, and well adjusted. Now that the eldest are growing up, I can talk to them on adult terms and it continually surprises me how quick and clever they are. But really, what I like best is just goofing around with them. We play on the Wii together and do all the dancing and they think it's hilarious that Grandma gets stuck in, busting out all the moves with them. I play games with the little ones and even love watching cartoons with them like *SpongeBob SquarePants*. I'm really just a big kid at heart. I'm so lucky to have this chance to enjoy my grandkids and I'm so proud of Toya and Zornae who are doing such great jobs as moms. I'm still working through a lot of stuff with Ricky and Zornae. These things take time but we're getting there.

Yes, I still bear the physical scars of my captivity – my hearing is still shot but I've learned to speak quieter now and although I like to have the TV turned up loud, I don't have any serious damage from the screwdrivers. I have some scars on my ankles from the chains and marks on my arms from where the boards cut them up. I don't cover them up. It is what it is. I can't change it. Taking away these scars isn't going to make my life any easier or make me forget what happened.

Since I've been in therapy with DJ things have got a lot better. The last three years have been the best of my life since I met Heidnik and although I've had setbacks I'm getting a little better at handling them each time. It's a constant struggle to make my life normal. No matter how ordinary and well-adjusted I may seem to people, very few see the turmoil underneath.

Mainly, what has kept me strong and provided me with answers is my faith in God. For a long time I struggled to understand why God would put a man like Heidnik on this earth and why He would choose me to cross his path. I know the answer now. He put me there to help get the other girls out alive. There was a plan all along and it was a positive one. Those girls needed to be saved because they would have never saved themselves. So I'm glad I was there and I'm glad I was mentally capable of saving them. I just wish everybody could have made it.

But am I the Josefina Rivera I used to be, before Heidnik? No. There was a Josefina Before and there is a Josefina After. The two are not the same. And that's okay. We all go through changes in our lives – it's just that some people's changes are more severe than others. For a long time I wondered how I was going to get back to the person I was before, refusing to acknowledge the change in me. I was stuck. And now, thanks to proper help, I realize there is no way back. You can't move backwards, only forwards.

So now I wake up every day and I look to the future. I look to what is ahead of me still and I feel very positive. These days I spend a lot of time helping out at the Salvation Army rescue mission, giving my time and energy to those less fortunate than myself. I'd like to do a counseling course one day so I can help other victims in a constructive way, the way that others have helped me. And Chris, who has been my rock and anchor through many troubled times, has asked me to marry him, so one day soon we'll tie the knot. I can honestly say I feel truly blessed with love.

Above all I just wake up every day and try to be the best person I can be. I try to be kind, helpful and heed my mom's advice. I'm not a good person or bad person but I try to be fair whether I like a person or not. My mom raised me to have values and that is something I've never lost.

And sometimes, when the feelings threaten to burst out and overtake me once more, I just like to wander along the beach, lose myself between the sand and the swell, and collect pieces of sea glass. Once lost, now recovered, these tiny fragments of the past come together in my jars at home, reformed from old structures into new shapes and pieces. Like the pieces of an unknown jigsaw, they take on new life and meaning on my windowsill.

They have survived. In some way, shape and form they have adapted, changed and survived. And sometimes, that is enough.

Acknowledgements

I would like to thank the following people.

DJ Schlag for his ongoing spiritual and mental support.

Pastor Weer and Chelsea Baptist Church for all their prayers and support, especially Cecelia Weer for her encouragement and friendship.

My children, LaToya, Ricky and Zornae, and my son-in-law Russell, for their love and support; my grandchildren LaQuoia, Bryahna, Jaaqwan, Sean, Gary and Princeton for their unconditional love.

The Lyle family for their help and support.

Dr Kavcavary and the entire staff at Atlantic Care Behavioral Health.

Charles Gallagher for standing by me in my time of need.

The staff of Special Victims Unit of the Philadelphia police department.

To my sister Iris Rodrigez who is no longer with us but is still watching over me.

Marvin Sapp for his inspiration from his song 'Never Could Have Made It'.

And finally, Kirk Franklin for helping me to remember I can smile.